Wearing a Mask Called Normal

One Woman's Journey From Abuse to Emotional Healing

AMRITA MAAT

TAKE
CHARGE
BOOKS

Brevard, North Carolina

Published by:
Take Charge Books
PO BOX 1452
Brevard, NC

**Library of Congress Cataloging-in-Publication Data
is on file with the Library of Congress.**

Copyright © 2013, 2016 Take Charge Books

ISBN: 978-0-9961589-4-7

Cover and interior design: Gary A. Rosenberg
Editor: Kathleen Barnes

Printed in the United States of America

This memoir is dedicated to the angels and spirit guides who have protected me throughout this life's journey. It is by the grace of the Divine that I have overcome a multitude of challenges. I have been given the gift of motherhood with three amazing children who have taught me valuable lessons. Each is a blessing, worth every challenge I have endured. It is with the guidance from the spirit world that I have evolved and become a healthier, happier and more authentic human being. For this I am eternally humbled!

Contents

Introduction

This story was born through the overwhelming sadness that I faced with the abrupt loss of a career that I believed was my primary life's purpose. With this loss came feelings of desperation and despair as I experienced total and complete isolation, shame and humiliation.

Much of this trauma I had suppressed for many years. My story re-emerged through therapy, meditation and personal desire for self-preservation. Each chapter reflects upon the bizarre dysfunction that I knew was abnormal, yet I concealed behind a facade created to preserve my self-esteem. I desperately desired to fit in, to be "normal."

My daily life was a staged act. I presented myself wearing a mask of "normal," knowing that my personal life was wrought with dysfunction and chaos. As my career abruptly ended, I faced silence and despair. It was my personal desire to face my abusers. I searched deep within myself to find the strength and determination required to overcome sexual harassment, bullying and mistreatment. Within my loneliness, this story emerged, with its theme of repeated emotional trauma and my personal healing.

I shattered my elbow during a hasty retreat from the sexual advances of a physician I worked with. This sudden and surreal injury changed my ability to perform my profession, my life's work, and had profound effects on my emotional and spiritual self. It was in that instant that my life dramatically changed as my physical body shouted, "Enough!" and forever altered the trajectory of my perceived life's purpose.

With this tragedy, I was taught through intuition and higher knowing how to protect myself in the future and to never be a victim again.

Many people are born into families that mentor them and provide them the life skills to protect themselves when they reach adulthood. I was never taught such skills. I was never mentored or trained how to defend myself from predators. The unfortunate result was a lifetime of poor choices, poor relationships and mistakes.

But we walk life's journey with many lessons along the way. For me, the lessons may be more dramatic than some and less dramatic than others, but they are *my* lessons. As I embraced faith and sought higher knowing, I overcame profound pain and birthed self-awareness. For these lessons, I am grateful.

It is through these lessons that I am. I am a daughter. I am a mother. I am a wife. I am a sister. I am a woman. I am a nurse. Never again will I allow another person to take any part of me.

I've written this book to share my story with others who seek answers on dark and pain-filled days. I offer you encouragement and healing strength.

Dysfunction, abuse and manipulation are not normal everyday behaviors. A healthy lifestyle comes first through recognizing unhealthy behaviors and then laying the groundwork for positive change. Positive change will vary from person to person dependent on individual circumstances. Lifestyle change that involves healthy choices must eliminate dysfunctional patterns that include manipulation and abusive behavior.

It was through my self-searching that I exposed my many

deficiencies and recognized how they repeated periodically over my young adulthood.

The metaphoric breaking point was my shattered elbow that led to a diagnosis of Post-Traumatic Stress Disorder. Intensive therapy, spiritual guidance and a loving spousal relationship have helped me transcend a lifetime of abuse. Meditation and prayer have heightened my intuitive knowing and my ability to communicate with the spirit realm.

It is said that as one door closes another will open when the time is right. For me, the door closed with a fury that shook my very soul. I experienced shame, humiliation and criticism as I searched for meaning behind the closing of that door. It wasn't until I learned the steps to forgiveness and devised *The Forgiveness Factor* that I was finally able to let go of control to a higher power and door after door began to open again.

I hope my story will open doors for you, too.

As you read, you will understand why I was forced to write the story of my journey under a pseudonym. It won't be a spoiler when I tell you that like many things in my life, the legal system failed me, seemingly precluding me from writing about my experiences without fear of legal retribution.

I assure you that every word in this book is true. Some details have been changed to protect me, the innocent.

—Amrita Maat

CHAPTER 1

Divine Intervention

"Yes Tom, it's true."

I paused as I watched his forehead wrinkle and his eyes widen under his metal-rimmed glasses. He scratched his head and repeated the same question: How did I injure myself and arrive in his office in search of care?

"I broke my elbow when I banged it on the wall in a delivery room," I explained.

He continued to gently twist and manipulate my arm as he examined it carefully, an x-ray reconfirming multiple fractures, then counseling me that this injury required surgical intervention.

"How in the world did you do that?" Tom asked as he immobilized my limp arm and attempted to distract me from the throbbing pain of my fresh injury.

Tom is an orthopedic surgeon and a colleague in whom I have deep faith and professional confidence. He has treated my family members from time to time for various sports-related injuries. This time I was the patient.

"I don't know how it happened, Tom," I answered, as I worked to create an alternate story to the truth that I did not want to share. I was ashamed and afraid to confess the repeated advances that I had been trying to avoid for the past few years. I was embarrassed that I could not work this situation out on my own, away from anyone's eyes. So, in disbelief and shame as the events from the previous evening replayed in my mind over and over again I repeated, "I really don't know."

However what had happened was completely preventable. As a nurse working on the labor and delivery floor, I have many years of experience and was preparing to take over the care of an already actively laboring woman. I was entering the labor room to introduce myself to the patient, unaware that her doctor was examining her.

This was a doctor I preferred to avoid as much as possible. He had been pursuing me for the past few years, despite the fact that he is married and so am I. As I was entering the patient's room expecting only the patient and her partner, I was thrust into a situation I was completely unprepared for. The doctor, Roger, was performing a vaginal exam to determine labor progress. The woman's eyes were tightly closed and she moaned in the distress of advancing labor and was momentarily unaware of her immediate surroundings. There was no one else in the room as the woman's partner had left to make a phone call.

Upon my entrance, Roger's demeanor changed as he became overtly happy to see me. Recognizing the patient's eyes were closed, he winked at me while licking his lips in a seductive manner. I was shocked! Taken back, I gasped and prepared to retreat from the room without spatial thought. In the instant that I made a sudden turn to leave, I accidentally slammed my elbow into the wall with significant impact.

The loud crack of my bone breaking resonated in the room. The overwhelming pain that followed almost brought me to my knees, but I tried to maintain self-control and not lose consciousness. All breath left my body as I desperately tried to maintain my composure and retreat as if nothing bad had happened. I briskly walked into the nurse's locker room to privately assess my injury. It took only a moment to realize it was serious and I needed to go to the emergency room right away.

"I was leaving the labor room to get something for the doctor and I slammed my elbow," I continued in monologue to the orthopedic surgeon. I maintained my story about an unfortunate accident, once again wearing my mask of normal, hoping to satisfy all questions and diffuse any possible suspicion.

Tom explained matter-of-factly that surgery was necessary. I had seemingly deterred any more questioning for the moment.

CHAPTER 2

My Beginning

*M*y mother was said to have "snapped" after my sister's birth. Maybe it was post-partum depression, but that didn't exist in textbooks back then. In reality, my mother could not cope with her life. She gave up. She didn't try for the good of her children. She went from doctor to doctor and was given prescriptions for anti-anxiety medications. They gave her pills and she slept all day. All day, every day, my mother slept.

Her way to cope was to sleep. When she was awake, she behaved like a manipulating child herself. Her manipulative behavior gave her freedom from raising a family without the shame of admitting that she just didn't want to be a mother.

Before I was five, I learned that my birth wasn't planned. The story went that my mother became pregnant by my father on her 18th birthday. She would often share with me her painful memories of my grandfather's shame and condemnation of her when he learned his daughter was unmarried and pregnant. She spoke of the punishments my grandfather imposed and how he kept her hidden in her bedroom for months. She was forbidden to leave the house when she was pregnant for fear that she would be recognized by people he knew.

The story of my shameful beginnings was replayed for me

several times over my early childhood, no doubt contributing to my sense of guilt for being alive.

My birth was not a proud and celebrated moment. I was told that I was born in the local Catholic hospital. It was the 1960s and, as I understood it, the nuns who operated the hospital worked tirelessly to try to convince my mother to give me to them. My mother described how the nuns didn't want her to hold me or be with me in the hospital. They believed it would be best that way. My mother did keep me and my parents married the month following my birth.

Dysfunction could have found its definition in our household in the early 1970s: A mother who spent every day impaired by Valium and a father who avoided reality by spending his days in isolation in the basement of the duplex home where we lived. My father had created a workspace in the basement that became his sanctuary from the irrational, manipulative woman he had married. He would leave us and hang out with his pot-smoking friends whenever the opportunity arose.

One of my strongest recollections of that time is my fear that he wouldn't return from these jaunts and my sister and I would be left alone with our mother. Before my mother's illness, my father was a blue-collar worker. He worked with a local union, but his job ended suddenly when my mother became extremely fearful of being left alone and he could no longer leave her side to fulfill his work obligations.

With no household income, poverty quickly fell upon us and we were supported through food stamps and family charity. Shame and embarrassment were compounded as we lived in a small town in rural Pennsylvania where privacy was compromised by small town living.

To call my mother abusive would be an understatement. The only childhood memories I have involve some form of emotional or physical abuse by her and my father rushing in to protect me. My mother's favorite form of punishment for me was beatings with the buckle end of a thick leather belt. She was merciless. With no tolerance for common childhood behavior, my mother would "fly off the handle bars" for the most trivial occurrences. Accidentally spilling a drink, leaving the front door open, not going to bed precisely on time were all fair game for my mother to grab the belt and induce fear, shame and physical pain on my being.

There were many occasions that I went to school wearing a plain Catholic school uniform that covered welts from the punishment of the preceding evening. But, I would pretend all was well, as I laid the foundation for my life by wearing a mask that made me "normal."

I recall many nights sleeping in the same bed with my little sister (we didn't have separate beds) with her rubbing my hair as I cried. She would tell me I would be okay. My 4-year-old sister would comfort me, the older sister, and try to make my pain go away.

It wasn't just physical pain that I endured. The emotional trauma seems even more damaging as I attempt to recover. One of my earliest memories was being told that my father might not really be my father. When my mother became angry she would find it necessary to share with me that it was "possible," depending on her mood sometimes it was "likely," that my father was not truly mine. So, in addition to the physical torment came the emotional turmoil of not knowing.

My sister and I were cocooned by dysfunction, phobias and abuse that wore us down from our earliest memories. We knew our lives were different from those of our friends, but we couldn't grasp the depth of wrongness. We never had sleepovers with friends. We never had play dates at our house. We left for school in the morning and pretended to fit in with our classmates. When we returned home to our reality, our pretend normalcy was left on the other side of the door to be reclaimed on another day.

Of the two of us, I was labeled the "difficult" child. My sister was much more passive and agreeable. She was better able to avoid causing the disruptions that so upset my mother. I was more active and more challenging. My mother interpreted my youthful energy and curiosity as being "difficult." Looking back on it, I guess I was "difficult" for her. I was unable to be a passive participant in my life or give my childish permission for my mother to sleep the days and weeks and months away in a state of emotional numbness.

So I endured the physical beatings, the welts and even a broken toe while my mother failed to cope. I became her punching bag, the target of all of her frustrations. I'm an adult now, but as I write these events, I can still feel the shame and pain of an innocent child, deep within my soul.

I spent my entire childhood accepting the label of being "the difficult child." I felt sorry for my mother and blamed myself for her problems. I believed that if only I hadn't been born, she could have had a better life. The story of my unwanted conception had been shared with me enough times that clearly my mother wished I had never existed. I believed I deserved her punishments. I was bad. I was worthless.

I clung to my father in my childhood. He played the role of both parents. He gave me sympathy and protection from my mother. He took his own abuse from her in the process. He succumbed to his own anxiety during these years, himself a victim of mistreatment and suffocation caused by my mother's manipulative behavior.

My parents' negative energies seemed to feed off each other and their fears and anxieties were synergistically fueled. The more debilitated my mother became, so did my father. They evolved into two phobic, crippled people who were incapable of providing a healthy nurturing environment for their children. It was inevitable that anxiety and fear would attach themselves to my sister and me. Could it have gone any other way?

My childhood sucked. My sister and I were drowning in this family life of addiction, fear, anxiety, child abuse and poverty. We struggled to support each other and hoped for better days. We were the collateral damage of this tragic relationship and we suffered. I mean we really suffered. Each new day brought uncertainty that came from having two parents who couldn't perform in those roles. We went to bed in fear and woke up in fear: fear of abuse, fear of physical pain, fear that our father would abandon us and leave us with her. These fears suffused our beings. We held each other at night for comfort and prayed together that we could have a normal family.

My parents separated when I was 10 years old. Actually, my mother left my father when I was ten. She blamed him for her problems and her illnesses, so she left my sister and me in his care. She would have taken my sister. That was understood. Not me, however. Her exact words were, "She is your problem!" before she drove off with my grandmother, who sat silently in the car.

This transition was tough. Our father struggled to provide for us while he remained overcome by his own anxiety disorders. He worked hard to re-assimilate in our community and find steady work. He took odd jobs, hustled and basically begged and borrowed to keep us fed and warm. An unfortunate accident soon after my parent's separation left my sister injured as a result of negligence on the part of our apartment landlord. My mother initiated a lawsuit in search of financial gain, which resulted in our being evicted from the home where I had lived my entire life.

Our father brought us to live with his sister and her family. I had escaped the physical abuse of my mother only to end up in an emotionally abusive environment that rivaled the previous one. My father was desperate to provide shelter for his daughters. He had no money, sometimes less than fifty cents in his pocket for a week. He had no choice but to bring us to live with our aunt.

We shared one room, my father, sister and I; just three twin beds in a small attic room. After a few weeks of witnessing me being emotionally tormented by my aunt, my sister begged me to go live with my mother. My mother was living in a one-room studio apartment in a motel next door to my grandparents. My sister couldn't tolerate the abuse and chaotic energy of my aunt. She saw no other option than to live my mother. She wanted desperately to remain with my father and me, but couldn't endure the instability and abuse of Aunt Phyllis. I declined.

There was no way I would survive living with our mother again. I would rather run away and live homeless than spend another bitter night with her. I would try to fit in with my aunt's family. I knew it was going to be difficult, but I would try to keep my distance and just focus on my studies.

Despite the suffering I endured in my private life, I was a good student. I learned easily and sought refuge from my secret world of abuse in my textbooks. I remained a straight A student.

We lived with my aunt a few months before my father was able to find us a new family member to spend time with. I was no longer able to hide my aunt's mistreatment from of me. Rather, my aunt became more relaxed and began to abuse me in front of my father.

She started to call me the hurtful names she once used outside his presence. She would make fun of me for clinging to my father and call me a "baby" for not wanting him to leave me alone with her. My aunt would laugh at me for spending so much time studying for school. At the time, I was in the fifth grade and her daughter was in the sixth grade.

As I continued to excel academically, despite the adversity I faced, my aunt was working with her daughter's school to get her permanently and legally released from mandatory education. My cousin didn't like school and refused to go. My aunt preferred to be her daughter's "cool mother" and supported my cousin's decision to leave school in sixth grade. She did leave school that year. Currently, my cousin is a crack addict and has had more than one stay in the county jail. I have a college degree and spend my days supporting laboring women. You be the judge.

Eventually, we did find a new apartment to live in. My father worked very hard to provide for me and protect me. My sister remained with our mother. My teenage years weren't without challenges. Dad found steady work and life somewhat stabilized. But I never had that mother support that helps when a girl begins to menstruate, or hugs of sympathy when she cries over the end of her first boy crush. I never had it. I didn't have a woman in my life that I could share a lunch with after a day of dress shopping. I envied all my friends who did. I struggled with my identity. I struggled with my self-esteem. I bounced from boyfriend to boyfriend searching for a normal relationship and a normal existence. I never shared my private experiences with anyone. Dysfunction, phobias and abuse were my secret life concealed within my soul and masked by my facade.

I am forever grateful for the love and support that my father was able to give me. He tried so hard to be both a mom and dad for me. He knew what I was missing and really did his best. We continued to struggle financially, but I was never without my father's wisdom and support. The wisdom he shared with me from my early days continues to resonate with me. I've shared my father's wisdoms with many young patients on several occasions.

When I was about 11 years old, my father tried to help me

to heal from the hurtful, abusive treatment of my aunt and her family. I couldn't understand how I could be ridiculed for liking school and doing well. My father tried to comfort me and ended that conversation with advice that has remained in my heart more than 30 years later. He told me I could be anything I wanted when I grew up.

"The sky is the limit," he said. "Follow your heart. Be true to yourself, and most importantly, always be able to provide for yourself."

He added, "Never, ever rely on a man to support you. Be able to take of yourself, just in case things don't work out."

This was sound advice from a loving father who spent every day just trying to survive for his daughters.

My dad did overcome his personal demons several years later. He now lives a modest life that is full of love and respect from his daughters and grandchildren. I am eternally grateful for his love and devotion that continued through his own personal struggles. He never walked away. He remains always supportive and always loving.

The horrible suggestion that my father is not truly my father has come up on more than one occasion in my adult life. My mother actually brought it up again in the past few years, despite adamantly denying its veracity for the previous 30 years.

Personally, I think it is very possible that my father and I may not be biologically connected. I will even go so far as to say that much of my mother's ill health is the result of the shame of creating a family life based on her willingness to deceive. However, my father and I have a bond that is forever created in a love that transcends biology. We agree that we don't need to know the truth. We don't want to know the truth. All that we have overcome together is truth enough for us.

During the early years of my mother's periodic hospitalizations and medical care, my mother was labeled *agoraphobic*. A person who is diagnosed agoraphobic has a pathological fear of open spaces. Victims of this disorder frequently are unable to leave their homes. She overcame this disorder by the time I was 20 years old when she went to vocational school, earned a degree and went from man to man looking for Mr. Right. Her addiction to pills continued.

She did eventually remarry, a man she met through a dating service. My sister and I knew it wasn't a relationship built on love and respect; rather it was another attempt to find someone to take care of her. That marriage recently failed when she once again fell into the patterns I remember from my childhood, sleeping all day, addicted to pills and living a life of dysfunction. She continues to deny that she has a substance abuse problem. She continues to repeat patterns of manipulation and deception.

When I'm in my mother's presence, the pattern of my childhood repeats itself. My sister, father and I have overcome and moved forward to the best of our abilities. Yet, my mother continues to regress, remains addicted and fails to overcome her demons. She failed me as a mother, failed my children as a grandmother and fails herself each day.

Fear has consumed most of my adult life: fear of loss, fear of failure and fear of abandonment. I carried these fears from childhood, despite my best efforts to shed them. My best metaphor would be to say I spent my life trying to shed the many patterns of fear that I had learned, like a snake that sheds her skin. I needed to shed these old patterns and grow new ones. It was a very long time before I was able to do so, a very long time.

CHAPTER 3

Exit Strategy

I needed to grow up more quickly than most ten-year olds. My father needed help taking care of my sister before she moved out, so I became the babysitter as well as housekeeper and cook. I swiftly adapted to these new roles. Looking back, I realize I never really was able to just be a kid.

My father worked long hours, frequently leaving me alone to manage the household responsibilities. I didn't realize at the time that I was missing out on my childhood. I naturally fit into my new prematurely adult role and honestly enjoyed my freedom.

I gave my father quite a challenge during my teenage years. I grew up fast. I was drinking by fourteen and staying out all night by fifteen. Although I was still a good student, high school was more of a social event than a place to study. It took me two hours to get dressed for school, making certain that my make-up and hair were just right.

Good grades were my last priority and, by the time junior year arrived, I just couldn't be bothered with classes. There seemed to be no challenge in school. None of it was interesting, even though I did plan on attending college. A few visits with the high school guidance counselor led me on a path to college that was much more fitting for me. It was a "bridge program" that allowed high school seniors to attend community college and earn credits for both programs. This certainly interested me as I saw no benefit in being in high school when I could be earning more meaningful college credits.

I worked out that process with my father's consent and attended community college during my senior year of high school. I also began to attend a local evangelical church and moved away from my pattern of drinking and staying out all night with friends. In hindsight, it is easy to see that I was desperately searching to fit in. I was trying to be normal. I never got caught up in drugs, legal or not, largely as a result of watching the ill effects of drugs on both my mother and my father.

Sometime during those years, I saw a palm reader who told me I was prone to alcohol abuse, so I shouldn't drink. I took her seriously and made a conscious effort to move away from that path.

I had found a new home in the church, with new friends and many older women who were willing to mentor me and be the mother figures they had recognized was missing from my life. Dolores, a woman who became a close friend, had a son my age who attended the same high school, so there seemed to be an early connection with that. I actively read the Bible during these days, stayed out of trouble and worked toward becoming the good Christian woman that I thought I was supposed to be.

It was during that time I met Gavin, the man who would become my first husband. He was the sound producer for a gospel-singing group that was pretty popular back then. He was setting up before a concert the night we met. His version was he was in love at first sight; I thought he was cute.

He was from the Bible Belt and I am not. We were instantly smitten and I think intrigued with our different accents and lifestyles. Our long distance relationship started that evening.

The church elders had been filling my head with their opinion that Gavin and I were meant to be together. It was God's will, they said. Gavin's mother had been married by the age of 15 and became a mother by 16, so I thought maybe they were right.

All I knew is that my life had sucked for pretty much its entirety and this man wanted to marry me. I remember thinking that if someone wanted to marry me, I probably should jump in. What if no one else came along? It was pretty narrow-minded thinking, but certainly not off the mark for a teenager. With the accepted marriage proposal came the end of my college career, at least for a few years.

We were engaged for three months while I planned a modest wedding with the help of Dolores, my church friend who was also my matron of honor. Because of the wedding, I missed final exams at college that semester and was given incompletes in all my courses.

After my wedding, I dropped out of college, obtained my GED certificate and was on my way down South to start my new life all within the space of a couple of whirlwind weeks. We were married just after my 18th birthday. Yes, married at the tender age of 18!

I spent the first half of year 18 on the tour bus or in rental cars travelling with my new husband. Gavin was 23. It all seemed pretty exciting then.

We settled in together in a pretty nice city in the Deep South. But, it was vastly different from my Pennsylvania hometown.

It didn't take long for me to recognize that I had made a huge mistake. I had taken the first bus out of my old life and plunged head first into a new culture, new life and new role, believing it was "meant to be." More than anything, I wanted to put my past behind me and go out and capture life. But I quickly realized this new life wasn't the life I had expected to capture.

In less than a year, I became extremely homesick. I missed the familiarity of my old life with my father. I missed my sister and my friends. I was not meant to live in the South, at least not at that time.

I recall the conversation with Gavin when I let him know that I was moving home. I told him he could come if he wanted to, but deep in my heart, I didn't want that to happen. I made preparations to return North and Gavin quit his job, reluctantly deciding to join me. I had prayed for him to make a different decision, but I was his wife and I had no choice.

We set up our lives in my hometown. I tried to carry on as a young wife, but really longed for my freedom. By the end of our second year of marriage, I wanted out more than words can describe. I just trudged through my life, watching life evolve for others while I remained stagnant in a relationship with a man I didn't want to be with. By the time I had turned 20, it was painfully clear that we were two very different people. Our cultures, values and evolving belief systems were more opposite than I could have ever imagined.

I wanted to return to college, buy a house and have a family, but not with Gavin. I longed for all the successes that I had seen my friends achieve. Gavin was content living in our rental mobile home and living in his status quo. We were completely mismatched and moving further apart every day. But I endured, more to avoid having to face my mother and admit I had made a mistake. I was going to carry out this marriage and never admit it wasn't working. I endured wearing my mask of "normal."

I lived unhappily for about five years, but I wasn't entirely spinning my wheels. I returned to community college when I was 21 years old, enrolled in a nursing program and finished my degree in two years' time. I excelled in college and started my nursing career at the local hospital. I was maturing, feeling alive when I was helping others. I was very proud that I was the first of my father's family to complete a college education. It was a proud time for me. But, it was bittersweet because as I continued to grow in my education and career, I was growing further away from the man I married.

By the time I was 22, I decided I had to get out of my marriage. I hated my life, again. I was beyond miserable. I had married at 18 when I knew no more about marriage and the meaning of "forever" than an old shoe does. I began to resent even the sight of Gavin. Several times in those five years, I tried to talk to him about our differences and my desire to go my own way. Each time Gavin would start to cry and beg me to stay. He couldn't accept what I was trying to tell him. He wouldn't hear me telling him that I needed my freedom; I longed for my independence.

His response was always the same: He would never let me go.

I felt trapped.

I continued this lie of a life, trapped and miserable. I kept on trying to love Gavin and to make our marriage work. Yet, as time passed, I became more bitter and angry. I began to resent seeing him and hearing him speak. He knew I was unhappy, so why wouldn't he let me leave? If he loved me, then how could he force me to stay in a space I didn't want to be in? It took many years for me to understand the answers to those questions.

My resentment and disgust grew as my marriage continued to dissolve. Finally, Gavin began to sleep on the couch while I struggled to reclaim myself. We basically became roommates, but I didn't have the courage to share what was happening in our home with my family and friends. Something within my core still didn't want to let my mother know that I had made a mistake, so I continued living a lie.

I kept this situation private as I formulated my plan for freedom. In the fall of 1988, I began to plot my exit strategy. Gavin and I were fighting daily. I didn't want to come home. It was at the point I just wished he would die. As terrible as that sounds, I felt this one person, my husband, blocked my struggle for freedom. I began to believe my only way out was through his death. Don't get me wrong. I wasn't plotting to kill Gavin, I was simply so trapped and so desperate for my freedom that I saw no other escape from my cage than his death.

New Year's Eve 1988: I was making secret plans to leave Gavin. I had decided my time had come. I had a good nursing job. I could provide for myself. I needed to be happy for once in my life. Gavin had been sleeping on the couch for nearly a year, so I had myself convinced he would be more accepting of this decision. Nevertheless, I kept my plans secret and plotted on. That evening, we had plans to attend a party at another couple's house to ring in the New Year. It was important to me to keep up the appearance that all was well, despite it being the farthest thing from the truth. I had a little too much to drink that evening and, to make a long story short, nine months later, Brandon arrived. I resolved to believe that this was the life that God intended for me. I tried to make the best of it. I truly did. I loved being a mom and Brandon became my new world.

It is amazing how unimportant other stuff in life became once I felt the love of my child. I was OK, at least for a while. Yet, as Brandon neared his first birthday, that gnawing ache for freedom began to fill my body and soul again.

I could do it. I could be a single mom. I had a good job. I could provide for us both and Gavin and I could arrange shared custody of our son. My plan seemed reasonable. Once again, I started looking for a place of my own, in secret, of course. I started calculating and working numbers to figure out how much living alone with my son would cost. I knew that I could not depend on Gavin to provide for us. My income was much more substantial than his. By Halloween of 1990, I found a place for us. It was just one month after Brandon's first birthday.

The time had come. I was going to be strong. I spent a few visits with a psychologist beforehand to help build my courage. I even asked Gavin to one of those visits to ease into breaking my news.

It didn't work. Gavin's reaction was explosive. But this time I was not going to back down. I spoke to a lawyer and prepared a separation agreement with joint custody. We had no assets and I was willing to provide for my son financially. Gavin refused to sign. He refused to discuss it. He refused to be rational.

CHAPTER 4

Abducted

I remember it like it was yesterday.

I left for work one Friday evening in the fall of 1990, shortly after I had told Gavin I was leaving. At the time, I was working the night shift from 11 p.m. to 7 a.m. so I would be home with Brandon during the day. Many nurses choose this path when they're raising small children. This type of scheduling flexibility is one of the appeals of being a nurse. About 20 minutes after I started my shift that night, my father arrived on the hospital floor. He was frantic. Dad had been staying with us for a few weeks and when he returned home, he discovered a most distressing scene.

Dad was shaking as he was trying to explain to me that Gavin's sister and her boyfriend were at our home with a rental truck and they were packing up Brandon and all his belongings and leaving. He had tried to call me from our apartment, but Gavin in a rage pulled the phone from the wall and broke it. There were no cell phones in 1990. In a panic to reach me, my father rushed to my workplace to tell me that Brandon was being taken away.

We left the hospital immediately. It took no more than 30 minutes for my father to arrive at the hospital, explain the situation to me and for us to return to my place. But it was too late.

The apartment was empty. Gavin had taken my son, his belongings and most everything he could pack in a hurry. The only thing that remained was Brandon's antibiotics in the refrigerator. He was being treated for an ear infection at the time. I was consumed with fear. This was not in *my* plan.

I called the police. I called my sister. I called my attorney. Reports were taken, but we had no idea which direction they were headed. To further fuel my panic, the police could not file a kidnapping report because Brandon was with his father. Gavin could technically take our son anywhere he wanted since we were married and no separation agreement had been signed. Therefore, the police couldn't stop him. It was out of their hands. With those words, I felt the breath leave my body. I just wanted to die.

My attorney told me that my hands were tied over the weekend until Monday morning when we could schedule an emergency hearing with the family court judge. By that time, it was the early morning hours of Saturday. Gavin had planned well by waiting for a weekend to take my son. This was certainly not a plan that he would have concocted on his own. Someone had counseled him on this choice.

I am at a loss for words to describe the fear, physical pain and heartbreak that I felt the moment I realized my son was missing. I had no idea which direction on this Earth they were heading and I could do nothing to rescue him before Monday morning. I felt dead. My existence would end until I had Brandon back.

Time literally stood still that weekend. Over and over, I called Gavin's parents begging and pleading for information about my son. All weekend long, they calmly denied they knew anything and continually hung up on me. Then they would take the phone off the hook for several hours so I would get an endless busy signal.

The very first time I called was certainly the most memo-rable. Gavin's father answered the phone. His voice was icy cold and full of hatred. I heard a combination of anger mixed with his personal victory as I begged for answers as to the where-abouts of my son. The monotone Southern accent was full of bitter smugness when he answered, "I have no idea what you are talking about," followed by, "You're as good as dead in Brandon's eyes now, so why don't you just move on?"

I think at that very moment all blood left the top half of my body and rushed to my feet. I went limp as I then realized that these people, Gavin's family, were planning on keeping my son forever. The phone line went dead, but those words in that evil voice replayed in my head over and over and over again.

Twenty years later, I still hear those words in my head with the same intensity of evil and hatred whenever I think of that moment. By the end of that and many other desperate phone calls to my in-laws, I began to feel comfortable that Brandon was on his way down South to Gavin's hometown. I knew I was in for a battle.

I stopped eating the night Brandon was taken. I couldn't eat. I couldn't sleep. All I could do was scream and cry all weekend long. I did take occasional sips of water at the urging of my father and sister. I knew that if I ended up in the hospital I might never get him back. But food was out of the question.

Monday morning finally came. I met with my attorney very early to prepare for an emergency hearing with the family court judge I came to know as Judge H. When Judge H. heard our problem, he immediately ordered Brandon's return to his home county. The only problem was that we had no idea where Bran-don was. This was the million-dollar question. More accurately, the $15,000 question because, in 1990, that is what it cost for me to locate my son and get him back.

Here is a brief history lesson about 1990. There was no

Amber Alert back then, nor was America's Most Wanted tele-vised in my area. The police were completely unhelpful and unsympathetic. The police advised me that Gavin did not break the law because Brandon was his son, too. Thank God for the compassion of Judge H. who became instantly agitated and joined my mission to bring my son home.

But where was Brandon? The next step was to hire a private investigator. My attorney recommended Mr. Franklin to help find them and get Brandon back. The going rate was about $500 a day. I was 24 years old, desperate and not able to afford that kind of money. I thought I was doomed. Fortunately, my grand-parents lent me a few thousand dollars and the search began.

Somewhere between Monday morning and Tuesday morn-ing after a few hundred calls to my in-laws' house, Gavin finally answered the phone. It was this moment that confirmed their location and the rescue operation could begin. Gavin told me that Brandon was fine and how he tells stories to him about me every day and shows him my picture.

"Oh, my God!" I thought. "This guy has lost his mind."

I was losing it, too. In that brief conversation, I begged Gavin to bring Brandon home. I begged him to not hurt Bran-don this way. I said anything I could think of to appeal to his son's best interest. It was like speaking to a stone. He hung up on me. I knew I had to get to that town quickly and get my son back.

I recounted the bizarre conversation with Gavin to Mr. Franklin and my attorney. I explained that Gavin believed he was going to keep me from my son and raise him as if I was just a memory.

Armed with the court order, Mr. Franklin began to prepare to travel to Gavin's hometown to retrieve my son. Judge H.'s order for Brandon's return was in compliance with the interstate child protection laws that were in place. Gavin's home state was one of many that had signed this agreement, so the law demanded that the child be returned to the state in which he resided. Therefore, Mr. Franklin expected this order would be upheld by this Southern state without delay.

I had a sinking feeling he was going to be wrong. I insisted I travel with Mr. Franklin, so we purchased two airline tickets South. Upon our arrival, we rented a car and headed into the small town where Gavin was raised and Brandon was being kept. Population 900. Maybe.

Mr. Franklin maintained that my son's transfer was going to be uneventful. The two states involved both had allegiance to the Interstate Child Protection Act and there was a responsibility upon those states to honor court orders.

Wrong! Little did we know that Gavin had reported to the local authorities that I was a child abuser and he was fleeing our home in search of protection. With his allegation, my clear-cut case instantly became mud. I was now a perceived child abuser and the local authorities were looking to arrest me. Yes, arrest me! I was in a very bad predicament. I was exhausted, starving and frantic as all these events started to unfold.

By the time Mr. Franklin came to the realization that we were getting the runaround from the local police, it was nightfall of Tuesday evening. Brandon had been missing for four days. I was closer to him geographically but still impossibly far from any resolution. It was the end of Day Four and I still didn't have my son.

To protect my anonymity, we secured hotel rooms approximately 25 miles from Gavin's hometown. Mr. Franklin was quite fearful that I might be arrested on a phony charge. He called Judge H. at home and advised him of what we were up against. From what I was told, Judge H. was very angry. He asked for the local judge's name and phone number and planned on calling him directly the next morning.

I recall Mr. Franklin trying to comfort me before I went to sleep. He wanted me to stop worrying about the money it was going to cost for him being on the job for several days. He was very compassionate and promised that it was his goal to return my son to me even if I couldn't pay. Mr. Franklin was enraged that local officials would be deceptive and dishonor an agreement between states designed to avoid issues like the one we were facing. I appreciated his kindness, but I didn't feel comforted.

Early Wednesday morning, I learned that Judge H. had spoken with the Gavin's local community judge. I also was dismayed to learn that Judge H. was getting the same runaround that we were. I knew I had to do something and I knew I had to act fast. Mr. Franklin and I drove to the local courthouse to continue the futile effort to get my son back through the legal process. He instructed me to stay in the car, lock the doors and duck down so I wouldn't be recognized. Mr. Franklin remained fearful that if I was identified in this town I would be arrested on a false charge. I promised to comply and stayed out of sight as Mr. Franklin locked the car doors and headed for the courthouse. The events that followed happened so quickly that all communication between Mr. Franklin and I ended until late the following day. No opportunity to explain my actions in private to Mr. Franklin ever emerged.

I was locked inside the rental car and obeying Mr. Franklin's instructions. As I stayed hidden beneath the view of passersby, I periodically peeked my head up in search of any sign of my son. In one of my brief moments gazing out the car window, I spotted my husband and father-in-law driving right past the courthouse. Gavin parked in front of a building a few hundred feet away and across the street. My mind raced! How could I just sit and hide when they were right across the street? I had to do something.

I had to speak with Gavin. I couldn't trust the legal system anymore. It was Day Five and my son was no closer to me than the first day he was taken by his vengeful father. The legal papers that were supposed to secure my son and return him to his home were no more valuable than the paper they were written on. I was from the North. Gavin was from the South, from the Deep South to be more precise. This was clearly a different world. This town was not just fighting me; it was still fighting the Civil War.

I had known for several years that the locals in Gavin's community did not much care for him marrying a "Northern Gal." But this took it to a whole new level of contempt. So, I did it. I got out of the car, walked across the street and entered the building my husband was in. It turned out to be his lawyer's office and I was standing square in front of the secretary. I calmly requested to speak with Gavin. She advised the lawyer that I was there and then directed me to his office. There I saw Gavin and his father sitting in front of the desk of a middle-aged dark haired man wearing wire-rimmed glasses.

I asked to be allowed to speak with Gavin and his lawyer, outside of the presence of my father-in-law. The lawyer accommodated my request and that moment I became an actress. I did not speak one honest word. I was the most desperate, believable and empty soul who would do anything in my power to get my son back. I did just that. I gave up my soul, my integrity and part of my innocence to reclaim my son. I have no regrets.

I began the conversation with Gavin and his attorney by telling them how sorry I was for this big misunderstanding. I told them both how much I loved Gavin and how I was mixed up and sorry for the undeserved pain that I caused him.

I explained that this was a family issue that needed to be resolved privately and not in the court system. Gavin's lawyer, of course, agreed and began quoting Bible references about marriage. After a little time passed, I asked if I could please speak with my husband privately. The attorney agreed this was a good idea and Gavin recommended we take a short drive to talk. I agreed and we headed about a mile out of town. Gavin parked the car. Within five minutes, we were having sex in the front seat as I proved my undying love for him.

It was vile. I felt like a whore. With each disgusting thrust, all I could think of was, "This will bring me one step closer to holding my son."

Thank God he finished quickly and we drove back to his lawyer's office. Problem solved. I thanked his attorney for his understanding and announced we were heading North to re-establish our family.

My father-in-law was not a happy man. More importantly, Mr. Franklin was astonished; he had been searching all over for me. His face literally became devoid of color. He had been working endlessly with Judge H. to resolve this matter. Those were too many failed attempts for me. I was finished waiting. I had taken matters into my own hands.

Gavin, Mr. Franklin and I drove the rental car back to my in-laws' shack and I was reunited with my son. I could feel life return to my body. I still hadn't eaten, but I was re-energized being with Brandon and feeling one step closer to victory. Victory in full meant being in my hometown with my son.

Brandon was filthy dirty. He was completely unkempt and walking around in a diaper that appeared to be from the night before. He was disgusting. The look on my mother-in-law's face when I walked in to her home was priceless. To add insult to her injury, I scooped up my dirty son, brought him into her bathroom, locked the door and took a 30 minute bath with my little boy. As I sat in the tub cleaning the dirt from my son and the lingering odor of intercourse with a man I truly loathed, I felt more power and more control in that very moment than ever before in my life. It was a baptism for Brandon and me, our new beginning. We were starting out clean and fresh. I was in control of this situation and f*** them all.

After the bath, we dressed while Gavin packed and headed out the door. Mr. Franklin made all the travel arrangements and we drove off for the airport. As we were walking to the car, I will never forget my mother-in-law saying to me in a low tone not intended to be heard by others, "If anything happens to my son, you will answer to me."

I responded in the same low and bitter tone, "F*** you," as I smiled sweetly and got into the car.

I ate en route to the airport. It was my first meal in five days. I couldn't get much into my stomach, but I did eat. By the time I got on a scale at home, I had lost nine pounds.

We arrived back at our apartment early Thursday morning. It seemed like a lifetime had passed since that previous Friday night. I slept a few hours with Brandon at my side. I awoke and continued my "happy wife" role as I dressed my son and told Gavin we were going shopping. I brought Brandon to a safe location. My attorney had already notified Judge H. that we had arrived safely home. Mr. Franklin was still unaware that I was playing a role. I was an actress. After bringing Brandon to my safe location, I spoke with my attorney and advised him that I had Brandon and I wanted full custody. There was a strange, silent pause on the phone.

Apparently, Mr. Franklin had informed my attorney and the judge that I was staying married. He had believed everything that he had seen and had believed it was my intention to reconcile. There had been no opportunity in the past day to let Mr. Franklin know otherwise. He let me know that I was quite convincing. It was at this time that I had to explain that if I didn't take matters into my own hands, this situation might not have ended in my favor. I knew that the legal system was not working efficiently despite everyone's best efforts.

Mr. Franklin, Judge H. and my lawyer couldn't believe what I had accomplished. A court hearing was scheduled about the same time I returned to my apartment to speak with Gavin. I was alone and the conversation was brief. I remember saying, "I'll see you in court," as I prepared to walk out on my old life forever. He stood there in shock and stared at me in disbelief. I left in haste, fearful that he might turn violent.

A year-long custody battle began when I left the apartment that day. In the end, Gavin lost custody of Brandon. The same day the judge ruled in my favor, Gavin moved back to his hometown and essentially abandoned his son. He has seen Brandon approximately six times in the past 20 years. I recently learned that Gavin's father passed away. The last words he spoke to me were, "You're as good as dead in your son's eyes, so why don't you just move on?"

I remember it like it was yesterday. Twenty years passed and I never received a call or card to apologize for his tremendously hurtful actions or words. He never saw his grandson again and lived till his dying day blaming me.

CHAPTER 5

Learning to Heal

I have no regrets about my choice to be a single mother. I rented a two-bedroom apartment and moved us into our new world, our new beginning. Gavin continued to create any roadblocks in his power to make this transition painful. Rather than engage with him in ridiculous battles over belongings, I decided to leave with just the essentials. I took my son and our beds. I left all the other furniture behind. Couches, tables, dishes remained with Gavin in my old world. They represented my past. I didn't need them or want them. Gavin did. So, he could have it all. He was welcome to all the furniture and the memories that remained. I wanted new beginnings. I had no desire and no energy to fight for objects that were replaceable.

My priority was happiness. This was the first time in years I felt that I was in control of my destiny. So, I had a big new apartment and no furniture to put in it. But I was happy. I recall the feeling of overwhelming joy as I set out to make a new life for Brandon and myself. I can do this. I can make this work. Let the journey begin.

Being a mom was my most important job. In order to spend as much time with Brandon as possible, I did what many nurses choose to do: I continued to work the night shift so I could earn money while my son slept. Then I would be home during the daytime hours when he was awake. It was very important to me to spend days with my son. For me, working nights was great for two reasons. First, it alleviated the guilt of having to go to work and leave my son behind. If I was working while Brandon was sleeping, I didn't feel like I was missing a huge piece of his development. Second, the night shift paid more per hour, so I could work fewer hours weekly to make ends meet. Therefore, I was able to be home more with Brandon.

This time in my life was a financial struggle. Despite court intervention, which obligated Gavin to pay child support for his son, I rarely saw any money from him. A few months after we separated, the court awarded me full custody of Brandon and with that decision, Gavin moved away. He emptied our old apartment and returned to his hometown, nearly a thousand miles from his son. He advised the court that this move was only temporary, but 20 years have passed and he has barely set foot in this county since. It was nearly impossible to enforce a child support order from that distance. I lived check by check and had little opportunity to save for the future, but that was okay because I was free from a destructive relationship.

Even though I didn't have any furniture, I did have a television and a VCR. Brandon and I would sit on the floor with large throw pillows and watch Disney videos together. It was a simple life, but simple was very sweet at that time.

I could not have survived during that time without the continued love and support of family. My father or sister would sleep over on the nights I worked to be with Brandon. I was fortunate that I didn't have to budget the additional costs of childcare on my salary given the exorbitant legal fees I was trying to manage. Brandon always had loving family members to watch over him and to support our transition from nuclear family to a single-parent family with lots of loving support. Most important, we were still a family.

Despite the distance between Gavin and I, the daily fear remained that my son would be abducted again. I had nightmares that involved Brandon being missing and I couldn't find him. I would call for him and my calls would become more panic-filled with each moment that Brandon did not respond. I would wake up in fear and run into Brandon's bedroom to find him asleep and safe. Each day of my new life challenged me with anxiety and fear that if I took my eyes off my son for a split second, he would be gone.

Surviving a child's abduction changes the family dynamic forever. I was consciously aware that I had just regained custody of my son through my own deception of leading Gavin to believe that we were going to remain married. Then, I was granted custody through the legal process. Yet the legal process did not give me any false hope of security. I understood clearly the limitations of the legal system and could not fully rely on it to protect my son if he was abducted again. It was a terribly frightening time for me.

Gavin was emotionally unstable. He had proven this by his previous actions. I had no reason to believe that he had regret for the pain he caused; rather he only had regret for believing in my sincerity and returning to our home. He was even more angry and bitter than he had been when he abducted Brandon. I clearly understood this. Each day of Brandon's young life I remained in a simmering state of fear, knowing that attempts to re-abduct my son were possible. I knew this fear was valid. It was because of this fear that Brandon became the victim of a more protective and sheltered life than most kids. By the time he was old enough for school, the principal and teachers would have complete legal documents on file to protect Brandon from any preventable events.

We teach our children at a young age not to talk to strangers and how to defend themselves against predators. Unfortunately for Brandon, he had to learn that he needed to be cautious if his father or relatives of his father approached him. I felt like my son lost a large part of his innocence because he had to learn that family might be unsafe too.

Yet to the outside world, I wore my mask of "normal." The mask that told people that I fit in and my life was no different from theirs. The mask I had worn from my earliest memories confirmed for me that my life was different, that my life was wrong.

CHAPTER 6

Fatal Attraction

*L*ooking out the window of my apartment one summer morning the following year, I noticed my upstairs neighbor leaving for work. My sister was visiting and we peeked through the blinds like a couple of high school girls watching him leave. We giggled and whispered about him and put imaginary bets on whether or not he was gay or straight.

We learned his name was Steve and that he lived with another guy in the apartment directly above mine. He was very handsome with dark hair and dark eyes, but his ethnicity wasn't obvious to us. Our guess was he had a Spanish background or some other Hispanic blend. He didn't seem to fit into my rural Pennsylvania community, but neither did I. I had lived in the apartment beneath him for a year, yet we never really crossed paths. I was going to change that.

One morning I watched out the front window, waiting for him to return home. I had a plan. I was going to open my front door to leave at the same time he was opening his front door to return. Brilliant! Masterful!

I was glad I thought of it. I had no clue what would happen next.

"Oh excuse, me," I said shyly.

"No problem," he replied.

I fumbled for something in my handbag and appeared out of sorts. "Do you need some help?" he asked like a gentleman. One thing led to the next and within days we were on our first date. Note to my sister: He is not gay.

Our first date was a movie at the local cinema. We had a good time and by the end of the night I was hooked, I mean completely blind-sided by what I believed was love. I had never felt that way before and I could not imagine my life without him.

We spent about the next year together; unfortunately it didn't take that long to determine we weren't meant to last. Somewhere in that year, talking became arguing. Steve was in his twenties like me and focused on building his career, not on settling down. I was dreaming about being a wife again and having another baby someday.

We broke up, we got back together and we broke up again. It was a roller coaster relationship with its ups and downs, but each time one of us got off the ride for some reason, we got back on. Eventually, we did separate completely. But, what neither of us expected hit us like a ton of bricks on my 26th birthday.

Still working the night shift, I turned 26 years old after midnight. My sister and a couple of close girlfriends from work were heading to a nearby bar to celebrate my birthday that evening. It was all planned. We were going to have a fabulous time full of potential to meet Mr. Wonderful. But, I didn't feel well that night. I was a bit nauseous and more tired than I should be, so I took advantage of one of my perks as a nurse, and sent my urine to the hospital lab for a pregnancy test. Surprise and Happy Birthday!! I was pregnant.

I was floored to say the least. Steve and I had broken up for good more than three weeks before. We just could not communicate. Now what? Happy Birthday to me! Twenty-six years old, single, still legally married and baby number two was on the way. WTF!

In my shock and disbelief, I decided to page Steve and make arrangements to discuss the news. It was about 2 a.m., but I knew he would be awake. He returned my call and was a bit more irritable than I had hoped for. I asked him if we could get together to talk, but he declined. I explained that it was pretty important, but he was already in a foul mood for whatever reason, so rather than beg for time I just blurted out my news, "I'm pregnant."

Silence . . . more silence . . .

Finally, after several minutes passed I said, "Are you there?"

He replied, in a painfully bitter tone, "What are you going to do about it?"

Quietly and honestly I responded, "I don't know." His last words to me at that time were, "Well, if you decide to keep it, you are on your own."

With that, he hung up the phone. I didn't hear from him again for more than a month.

In retrospect, it is completely understandable why Steve and I could not get along. He was focused on himself and was not in a place in his life where he wanted to be distracted with a relationship. I wanted him to realize that dream, but I also wanted to be part of the picture.

We really were at two very different places in our lives. Living so close to each other also added some stress to the relationship because from the beginning, we spent nearly all our free time together. We did not have any buffer distance between us. This really did create strain early on in our relationship.

However, we were truly very different people. Steve's values were different than mine. I tried to shift my values to conform to his, but obviously this behavior is doomed from the onset. In all honesty, we had nothing in common except for sex. As long as we didn't need to speak with each other we got along fine. In the bedroom, we weren't talking.

The month with no communication from Steve was a difficult one. But, after much prayer and internal struggle I decided I was keeping the baby. I had no intention to cause Steve any pain and I had no intention to trap him in a loveless relationship. I did intend to keep this child and do the best I could in the situation.

My mother learned about my pregnancy through the family gossip chain soon after I made my choice to keep the baby. I did not receive a call of congratulations or support in my decision, rather I heard third-hand that my mother's response was, "She's not keeping it is she?"

So, the lack of motherly support in my life continued. I was facing a new challenge and trying to do the best I could in this situation. Once again, I was on my own.

Internally, I heard a voice over and over again telling me it was shameful to have two children by two different fathers, especially, since Gavin and I were still legally married. I felt embarrassed and ashamed that I was carrying a second child by a father who would not give me the time of day. But, I tried my best to maintain a positive view. I had a good career and I was going to be a mother again. I did resign myself to the reality that I was going to be a single woman for quite a long time. In this situation, I would not be able to buy a date.

I wish I could say that I left Steve proudly and stood on my own two feet. But the devastation of being alone, in combination with the pregnancy hormones, really turned me into a desperate and pathetic person. On more than one occasion, I reduced myself to begging him on my knees not to abandon me and to please be supportive. I recall like it was yesterday the emptiness in his eyes when for the last time he shut his apartment door and ignored my cries. I spent the remainder of my pregnancy in shame as I learned that he was dating someone else while I was carrying his child.

When I learned that Steve was dating again, despite our situation, I realized just how disposable my unborn child and I were to him. Steve had moved on, but I was stuck.

Equally painful was the knowledge that another woman would actually become involved with a man who was so viciously unsupportive of his pregnant ex-girlfriend. I think that was even harder for me to process at the time. To me, women are supposed to uplift and support each other. It is some kind of unwritten code. I couldn't understand how another woman would want to be with a man who was openly and consciously rejecting another woman who was in a vulnerable position that he helped create.

However, through this experience I began to see with more clear vision just how cutthroat women can be to each other. All women do not share the unwritten code I believe in. This would not be the first time I learned this difficult lesson. I think that this experience may have unconsciously contributed to my desire to attend to women as a nurse, to uplift and support them, rather than tear down or weaken.

In order to prepare for my additional upcoming expenses, I moved into a smaller, more affordable apartment. I had no financial help, so I needed to exercise as much caution as possible to remain solvent. It was probably also better to remain physically distanced from Steve.

Brandon and I settled into our new apartment well and watched my belly grow with each passing day. Brandon was excited he was going to be a big brother and we would speak daily about his responsibility to love and protect his brother or sister. Our new arrival was expected right around Brandon's 5th birthday.

Obviously, Steve and I would have failed miserably if we chose to stay together. This pregnancy was not one of love, support and joy, but it was mine and I embraced my unborn child with anticipation and desire to be a good mother. My circumstances were far from ideal and brought with them shame that I had gotten into this situation. But all of this was tempered by the joy of being a mother again. With each new day of this anticipation, I wore my mask of "normal" and pretended all was well.

I held on to a fantastic notion that one day Steve would change his mind and recognize the error of his ways. I prayed that he would contact me and profess his love for me and his desire to be a family. Eventually, he did, but by then it was far too late.

CHAPTER 7

Seeking Mystical Guidance

I went to see tarot card readers a few times during my second pregnancy. Actually, I consulted two different tarot card readers and compared their predictions. Both were great ladies and I appreciated the kindness and sensitivity they gave me as I sought direction and hope for my future.

I was looking for confirmation that Steve would come back to me and we would be a family. I remained hopeful that if I gave him the space he needed to process this life's change, he would realize his mistake and return to me and our child.

The clairvoyants did not confirm that my earnest wishes would come true. The prediction was I would date and possibly marry a man named David. They also predicted that as I moved on with my life and was no longer interested in Steve, he would return and want to reunite with me. They insisted that this man named David was someone I already knew.

I wracked my brain trying to figure out the identity of this David person whom I might one day marry. I drew a blank.

Steve was not going to be the one, the readers said. By that time, I was six months pregnant and desperate for hope that Steve would return and my intolerable situation would improve.

I meditated on these predictions and continued with my

daily rituals in anticipation of change in the near future. I waited for David to reveal himself to me, believing from that moment forward that David's emergence would be the best chance that Steve would want to reunite with me.

When I returned home from my readings, I shared the news of my predicted future with my sister. Both of my psychic counselors allowed their sessions to be taped, so I could play the tapes and my sister and I would do our own self-assessment of the messages. We maintained watchful waiting, but I swore I did not know any man named David.

One day at the nearby grocery store, I was picking up a few things for dinner. I was well into my eighth month of pregnancy. I was large and quite awkward as I waddled through the aisles. As I approached the checkout line I heard a familiar voice greeting me, "Hey Amrita, how are you doing?"

I turned to my right and in the next checkout aisle was a guy that I had seen at the gym before I stopped working out due to my advancing pregnancy.

"Oh, hi, David," I responded and answered that everything in life was status quo.

David lacked subtlety as he gave me the full body scan that largely focused on my growing belly. "Wow, you are big!" he noted, giving voice to the obvious. This was the best response he could come up with at the moment?

I smiled politely, thinking sarcastically, "Brilliant! Very well put."

But I understood there was no malicious intent. David was a very nice guy. So, I remained pleasant and told him that I was nearing the end of my pregnancy.

We spoke for several minutes while we waited in line and we were quite surprised to learn that we both were living in the same apartment complex. He was living on one end and had moved in recently. I was living on the opposite end and had also just moved in. Before leaving the store, David asked me for my apartment number and wished me the best of luck with the upcoming delivery.

Not once did I connect the psychics' readings with this chance meeting. I felt no physical attraction to him and I would expect him to have no physical attraction toward me in my current state. Not unless he had a screw loose, of course.

Within a week of running into David at the grocery store, I returned home to find a gift bag hanging on the doorknob. The gift inside was neatly wrapped. As I entered my apartment and placed my belongings on the table I wondered who would leave me a gift. I opened it carefully. It was a book. *The Emotionally Abused Woman* written by Beverly Engel with no card attached. Who would leave this book for me and why? My sister showed up and, putting on her detective cap, was determined to solve the mystery. She began to flip the pages in the book and the sender became apparent. The sender had written the most thoughtful and considerate message inside the front cover. It was David.

David! The puzzle pieces began to fall into place in my mind.

"He likes you," my sister smirked.

"Don't be an idiot!" I snapped back defending his honor, "He is just trying to be a nice guy." I called him to thank him for his kindness. I told him that I appreciated his thoughtfulness and would let him know when the baby arrived.

Within a few weeks, my daughter arrived. I named her Celeste, Latin for heavenly. After returning from the hospital, I made a few phone calls. I called David who congratulated me and we discussed a few details about the birth experience. A few minutes into the conversation, David invited me to join him and a few friends to a football game in a few weeks. I thanked him for the offer, but wasn't sure if I could accept with a brand new baby. I told him I would have to get back to him before I could commit.

"I told you he likes you!" flew out of my sister's mouth before I barely hung up the phone. She then offered to watch my children, so that I could go to a football game, get out of my apartment and have a little bit of fun.

My sister encouraged me to make plans. "You need to get out and have some fun, Amrita. Just go."

It felt wrong to go out and leave my new baby. I remember feeling like I didn't deserve to have fun. I was a mother and my children needed me. They didn't need a babysitter while I took off to a football game and left them behind. My sister whole-heartedly disagreed and fervently encouraged me to call David and accept his invitation.

So I did.

It was autumn and I was off to my first football game. It was an absolutely gorgeous fall day, one that I hope to never forget. David picked me up and we met the other couples at the game. I had a great time, despite the feeling that all eyes were on me, the single woman who just had a baby two weeks ago, wearing her mask, pretending to be normal while trying intently to cover the shame she wore on the inside. I was self-conscious, but I worked through my insecurities and remained pleasant, hoping for a good day. By the end of the game, I was very happy that David had asked me to join them. We returned to my apartment and he met Celeste for the first time. He even asked to hold the baby. David held this tiny newborn baby with natural gentleness. I appreciated his kindness and thanked God for the new friend.

CHAPTER 8

Times of Healing

David and I began to see each other more frequently after that first football "not-a-date" in October. We began to go to dinner on weekends and talk on the phone several times a week. We weren't dating in any official capacity. I liked him. I just didn't like him in that way. You understand, the *sexual* way.

I was still recovering from Celeste's birth, so taking sexual interest in any man was not on my list of important things to do. But I definitely enjoyed David's company. He had a natural way of taking my mind off of my everyday stressors and just bringing me simple happy times again. I appreciated that.

David will tell you that he was not the physical type I was generally drawn too. He pointed out to me that I was naturally drawn to dark-haired, dark-eyed men. I had never paid attention before, but he certainly saw my pattern and he was right on the mark. David is light-haired and light-eyed with a significantly thinning hairline. I suppose in hindsight the fact that he was losing his hair in his thirties was something that was not attractive to me at that time. But, I enjoyed his company and we continued to be friends.

I recall during this same time, Lynn, my girlfriend's mother, tried to fix me up on a blind date with a guy named Al. She sang praises for this guy she worked with and thought he was, "just my type." I had never been on a blind date before, but my girl-friend talked me into it.

I met this guy for dinner. He was a sheriff in our local jail. All I can say is first impressions truly do speak volumes. He was very tall. I suppose near six feet five inches or more with light brown hair and a few teeth missing when he smiled.

"Ugh!" I thought. "I am going to kill Lynn when I see her."

I remained pleasant through the meal and declined dessert. I felt so bad for Al and his hard luck story about paying alimony for four children that I gladly bought my own meal. I just wanted to get out of there.

Throughout my ride home, I kept thinking of David and wondering what he was doing. This was the first time I realized just how much I missed him when he was not around. Rather than heading straight home, I went to David's apartment first and gathered up my nerve to knock on his door.

We weren't dating so I felt awkward knowing that he might be with someone else. He was alone. He answered the door and asked me how the date went. We both laughed as I shared my first and last blind date experience. Then, I did it. I told him how much I missed him and how I thought of him throughout the entire meal. He looked at me, smiled (with a full complement of teeth), and in that moment, he kissed me. It was really nice.

It was close to three months of dating/not-dating, so still no sex. I was not ready to make that commitment again, especially with the baggage of my background. I just could not bring myself to risk being hurt again. I liked David. I liked him even more than I had anticipated, but sex brings a relationship to a whole different level. I just did not feel prepared for that.

He never pressured me. Not once. We enjoyed each other's company and somehow evolved into not dating other people, but sex wasn't happening . . . yet.

People who watched television in the early 90s will recall

that *90210* and *Melrose Place* used to air consecutively once a week. My sister and I never missed the episodes and even had our own ritual of talking to each other on the phone for nearly the entire two hours. During one of these mini-drama nights, my sister and I started a discussion about sex and she reminded me that it had been several months since I had any. We were laughing and carrying on and being sisterly stupid when she starting suggesting to me that I should go knock on David's door and "do it." We laughed at the thought of it, but I rejected the idea and told her it wasn't happening. My sister remained persistent and asked me what I had to lose.

"Go ahead and just do it. It's been a long time," she continued.

So I started thinking and finally agreed to go for it. Really, what did I have to lose? Well, I answered myself, I could lose my self-respect. Again.

In our master plan, we agreed that my sister would come over to my apartment to babysit and I would go to David's apartment during commercial break with the intention of "doing it."

Commercials started when my sister arrived. She wished me luck and I was out the door. I only had about six minutes before the show began again, so I was in a hurry.

Knock, knock, knock.

"Hey, what are you doing here?" he asked as he answered his door. "No time for small talk," I thought to myself as I kissed him, no more words necessary. He got the hint.

Jackpot! We did it.

"No time to discuss now, the commercials are over, got to run. Bye."

With that, I was out the door and back to my apartment. I looked at my sister with a big cheesy smile.

"Did you do it?" she asked. I just nodded and no more was said.

CHAPTER 9

A *Magical Season*

*D*avid and I continued to date and in less than six months, I was hooked. It was one of the snowiest winters in our area in many years and David and I were together most of his free time. Our nights were spent watching the snow fall and planning our future together.

It was truly a magical season for me, a season filled with very special memories. My children were thriving, my personal life was changing for the better and I was no longer crying every day. I was smiling. Steve had been absent from the time of Celeste's birth and it just didn't matter. Actually, at that moment in time, I was relieved he wasn't around. My life was once again in a place of healing.

One snowy night, David and I had returned from a fabulous dinner and it seemed we connected in a deeper way. That night our relationship transformed from simple sex to making love. I went into the living room to put on the Late Show and as I looked back toward the bedroom I caught a brief glimpse of David as he walked naked toward the bathroom. He was very fit and for the first time, I saw him in a more intimate and loving way. I remember thinking at that very moment, "I could get used to this."

Fast forward nearly 20 years: I still feel the same way.

If you ask either one of us who proposed, we don't know. We really don't recall how our dating transitioned to an engagement, but it did and one day we were planning our wedding. I do remember being adamant that I could not live with him without being engaged. I was not comfortable bringing my children into a live-in environment with another man if I wasn't getting married. David respected that and we did eventually move in together as our wedding preparations were under way. At the time, we hadn't exactly decided on an engagement ring, but our wedding plans had begun. After we made love to christen our very first night together in our new living space we snuggled up together and began to speak about what the next day was going to bring.

As we started to outline our future, David took my left hand and placed the most gorgeous diamond engagement ring on my finger. It was exactly the one I wanted. It was the very ring I showed my mother one day when we were shopping at the mall. Her devastating response: "What makes you think you deserve something like that?" It cut through my very soul.

Thankfully, David thought I deserved it as he smiled and gently told me that he didn't want me to spend one night living with him without being officially engaged. He made sure I was wearing an engagement ring before I went to sleep in our bed for the first time. My future husband, the romantic.

Our wedding was set for autumn the following year. David and I worked within a budget and plans were going well. I only had one minor detail to correct by then: I needed a divorce.

Years had passed and Gavin still refused my repeated requests for a divorce. Gavin knew nothing about my second pregnancy, my wedding plans or anything about his son. He just refused to divorce me. We had no assets, so it wasn't about money. I had left the majority of the furniture and our belongings with him the day I moved out. Gavin simply refused to let me go.

My attorney had a big undertaking ahead of him to secure my divorce in the seven months before the wedding. David was very concerned, but I kept telling him not to worry about it. Of course, he didn't completely believe me.

A court date was finally set in the state Supreme Court in August, just one month before my wedding to David. I kept my fingers crossed despite the fact that my attorney had warned me it might still take several months for the judge to sign divorce papers even after the trial. I carried on in faith that everything would be okay.

In the meantime, my attorney attempted several times to settle the divorce stipulations before the actual trial date, but Gavin wouldn't budge. As the process unfolded, it was determined that Gavin was in arrears close to $15,000 in child support for Brandon. He had not paid anything for the years we had been apart and he was now in debt to me for a large sum of money. In order to secure my divorce, Gavin wanted me to waive that dollar amount in exchange for his promise to not contest our divorce any further.

I thought about it. I discussed it with David. My final decision was to agree to Gavin's extortion. I had to face the fact that Gavin was a deadbeat dad, and I took some small comfort knowing that he had to go to sleep at night knowing that. I had been providing for my son all these years and never had any belief that I was going to actually see that money anyway. So, I agreed and went before the judge in August to finalize my divorce. The proceeding was uneventful until the very end when my attorney spoke to the judge.

"Oh, one more thing, Your Honor," he said, "My client has a wedding planned in one month, so we respectfully request that Your Honor sign these papers as expeditiously as possible."

The judge's eyebrows raised and his face contorted just a little bit as he responded, "I'll see what I can do."

The divorce papers were in my hand ten days before my wedding. I did it!

It is important for me to share another event on the day of my wedding. I was lying in the bathtub, trying my best to stay relaxed as I prepared for the amazing night that was ahead. The children and David were not home and I had created a peaceful space for the few hours that led up to the more chaotic wedding preparations with hair, makeup, dress, etc. This was really the first quiet moment I had in months. As I lay in the soothing warm tub planning the rest of my day, the telephone rang.

"Hello?" I asked as I sank into the bubbles.

"Amrita?"

I recognized the voice on the other end instantly. My heart immediately sank. It was Steve.

"What do you want?" I asked reluctantly anticipating trouble knowing that he was calling on that specific day.

"I don't want you to get married," he said very quietly, almost in an adolescent voice.

"I think you need to reconsider it and not get married," he added. "I've been thinking about it and I think we should talk about being a family."

He paused and waited for my response. My head was spinning. I couldn't believe these words were really being spoken.

I was silent for quite a while before I finally replied, "I am getting married in less than six hours."

In this brief moment of contemplation that seemed like an eternity, everything that I thought I once desired was being offered to me. The psychics were right: I was faced with the decision that I cried and prayed for endlessly during my pregnancy with Celeste.

"Good bye Steve," I softly said as I hung up the phone and cried in my bathwater. How dare he? I thought. Why now?

David and I were married that evening. It was nearly one year after the football game. As we stood before God, family and friends and recited our vows, David promised to love me and my children. I still don't fully understand why he would take on this burden, but more concerning to me was whether or not I was going to be able to keep my secret from him. I am not normal. My life is not normal. I wear a mask of normal, but I was fearful what would happen if he found out it was all a facade. I was grateful for his love, but spent my days fearful that he would learn my horrible truth.

CHAPTER 10

New Challenges Begin

The adjustment to married life was not without its challenges. In addition to being a new wife and mother to two young children, I had returned to college with the goal of advancing my nursing degree. I wanted to work on a labor floor, but for that, I needed more education and experience. I had never given up my childhood dream of supporting women and empowering them in the birth process. When I was a little girl, I was the labor coach for my pet tabby cat as she delivered her kittens. I wanted to coach women with human babies.

This goal would require two consecutive years of additional college to finish my undergraduate studies. I had made the decision to return to school before David and I were engaged. He remained supportive of me and stood behind me every step of the way. Yet, this was a tough time. Each of us was adjusting to being part of a new family unit. Brandon was six and Celeste was a year old when I married David. We bought a small home and everyone was adjusting nicely to our new family life. Life felt good.

Celeste was growing out of diapers and breastfeeding around the same time I began yearning for another baby. I can recall a deep aching within my ovaries to have another child. As Celeste became more and more independent, the more I wanted another baby. It was a warm summer day and David was outside doing yard work as I approached him to ask if we could have another child.

"Do you think we could have another baby, PLEASE?" I asked with a grin on my face that I suppose David could interpret as either joking or serious at that moment.

"What?" he asked as he continued to whack weeds along the perimeter of the house.

I repeated the question.

"I don't want to talk about this now," he answered, ending the conversation for the moment, but I knew he would come back to it for me.

Later that evening, David offered several legitimate reasons why having another baby was not a good idea. Money, time and hard work were included. He couldn't appreciate the innate hormonal drive that was motivating me and although he was never hurtful, he wouldn't concede. The subject ended, but only temporarily.

Over the next few years, I periodically returned to my desire to have another baby. It seemed I just couldn't give up. I really wanted another baby. By that time, I was in the home stretch of my college studies. I was reaching my thirties and feeling internal pressure that if I didn't have a baby soon, I would likely lose the opportunity to my biological clock. So, I persisted with David and brought up my same argument several times a year.

"Please," I would plead as tears rolled down my face. "Just one more baby?"

He remained firm with his one syllable answer, "No!"

I would walk away, defeated again.

Finally, after my years of trying unsuccessfully to persuade David, we were sitting in a local restaurant on a Saturday night I said jokingly to him, "You know I am ovulating?"

With that, I truly expected some form of a sarcastic response intended to change the subject without hurting my feelings once again. David just sat there eating his meal. It seemed like several minutes passed before he spoke. Then he looked up at me and smiled and said, "Okay."

With that, dinner ended without dessert as I hastily asked for the check. This was the first time he had agreed to try to make a baby and I wanted to get him home to bed before he changed his mind.

I will never forget that night. We made a true attempt to start a new life together while Marvin Gaye played *Let's Get it On* in the background. For me, as much as I adore my two children, it was my first time to create a life willingly and not within circumstances that I didn't control. That evening was one of many special evenings I have shared with my husband.

When we had finished, in the typical David fashion that I cherish each day, he got out of bed and said, "That ought to do it!" as he proceeded to the bathroom.

I smiled and lay still hopeful that he was right and in a few weeks we would share some very special news. I had never tried to get pregnant before, so this moment for me was part of my healing from the dysfunction that had long been part of my life. It symbolized a transition to my new life of "normal." I had worked for it.

David loved me enough to be a wonderful father to his stepchildren and finally he had agreed to bring forth a new life with me. I was bathed in love that I had never experienced before.

Several months passed with no new pregnancy, fuelling my suspicions that something wasn't right. I was becoming more knowledgeable about women's health in college and developed concerns in my personal life. I was worried that there was something wrong with me, so I sought counsel with my gynecologist. Success finally came with the assistance of medication that increased my egg production and more targeted intercourse that was monitored through blood work to determine the precise day of ovulation.

By April, David and I learned we were pregnant—with twins! The pregnancy was confirmed by ultrasound and we were in shock, but not unpleasantly so. We returned home to tell the children our family was growing. I was ecstatic!

CHAPTER 11

Baby Heartbreak

The pregnancy was going well and we were both adjusting to the notion of two babies coming home. We were having practical conversations about cribs, strollers and making decisions about buying a minivan.

I was not happy with the idea of a minivan. I did not consider myself the "minivan mom" type and I really was looking for a better solution. By week 15 of my pregnancy, I was off to the doctor for my ultrasound and check-up. I couldn't wait to see a picture of my growing babies and hear the updates. In a million years, I never anticipated I would receive such horrible news.

It appeared that one of the twins was extremely and significantly deformed. The deformities did not follow any specific genetic condition like Down's syndrome, but the doctor gently informed me the defects were "incompatible with life."

In other words, the baby might survive inside my body, but it would certainly not survive outside. My head spun as I digested the words. I literally felt like the life was being sucked out of my body as I tried to comprehend that I was going to lose the baby that I had not yet met.

"Isn't there something we can do?" I pleaded for answers and repeatedly suggested a mistake must have been made, even though in my heart I knew there was no mistake. My doctors were very experienced and they were much more knowledgeable than I was. My baby, our baby, was not well and decisions needed to be made quickly.

These decisions involved protecting our other unborn baby. He seemed quite perfect, but the doctors warned us that there were risks to his wellbeing as a result of being in the same environment with his unhealthy twin.

David and I were bombarded with discussions and options about pre-term labor and genetic diseases. One thing I did know was that there was no way a child of mine was going to become a hospital experiment. If my child's deformities were truly incompatible with life, then I wasn't going to risk him living for even a few moments and becoming a scientific experiment that ultimately would delay his inevitable death.

Working in medicine exposes health care workers to a more complete understanding of the tragedy that often comes with dying in a medical facility. Dying in a hospital involves machines and intravenous tubes with fluids and blood being drawn intermittently.

An ill newborn is not going to be allowed to die peacefully. Instead, there will be a grueling and painful attempt to preserve and prolong the inevitable. I personally couldn't bear to see it happen if I knew for sure that my child truly had a terminal condition. That being understood, we had only two options.

Option 1: Do nothing. Let the pregnancy and the circumstances play out as they would.

Option 2: A doctor in Manhattan had recently developed a technique that was designed for reducing multiple pregnancies down to a more manageable size. Basically, women who were pregnant with several fetuses could opt to reduce down to maybe a triplet or twin size. The technique was quite new, but was promising hope for women in tragic situations like ours.

David and I made an appointment to talk with this physician. We didn't know what to expect, but we needed to learn more about this procedure.

The doctor called it "selective reduction," a specialized procedure that can bring a multiple pregnancy down to a safer gestational size. It was very new at the time I was pregnant and had only been done a handful of times. With the circumstances we faced, we needed to be absolutely sure that our child did indeed have the significant anomalies that were being described. So, we wanted absolute confirmation that our baby was not going to live outside of my womb and would likely die soon and threaten his healthy twin.

After careful discussion of our expectations and multiple tests completed by the doctor, he confirmed the worst. With much prayer and so many tears, David and I agreed this might be our only chance to protect both babies. We saw no other option that suited our spiritual and personal values, so we proceeded to the next step with complete faith in the doctor.

The whole experience was terrible. This many years later, as I write about it, the tears come to my eyes and my heart aches. We never discussed with our families the details of what we experienced and the choices we faced.

To this day, they are unaware of the specifics of our personal challenge that strengthened us as a couple, but could have easily broken us. We endured a heart-wrenching death of a child we were unable to hold, but were able to see by ultrasound. Time and time again, we saw the birth defects that were pointed out to us before we made our decision. We loved our baby just as if he was as perfect as the first snow of winter. We loved him, we wanted him, but more than that we couldn't bear thinking of him suffering even if only for a few moments.

We saw his brother, who appeared to be healthy and thriving and we loved him just as much. We grieved the loss of one son as we celebrated the growth of another. It was a bittersweet day filled with tears and sorrow. It was the day we watched our son's heartbeat stop on the ultrasound screen. God forgive me! I love him, please bring him home to you that I may see him another day.

CHAPTER 12

Christmas Present

My third pregnancy was not as I had anticipated after the reduction was completed. Soon after, I began to have regular frequent contractions that were placing me at high risk for preterm delivery. To prevent this from occurring, I was instructed to remain on strict bed rest, given medications daily and strongly advised to avoid all sexual activity for the remainder of the pregnancy. This totaled about sixteen weeks.

These restrictions brought with them additional challenges that affected my entire family. I was still a nursing student with only months till graduation and the result of this setback was going to delay my completion of the program. Brandon and Celeste were still young enough that they needed their mom to be actively involved with them and not just a lump in a bed. It reminded me of my mother's marathon sleeping. I didn't want to be that to my children.

Once again, David was burdened by increased family responsibilities that included being caregiver for me as well as the children. Overall, the pregnancy that in my mind offered promise of being "perfect" relative to my past pregnancies was not turning out the way I had planned. Each day I feared that day might be the one that I lost our child. Each day I lay in bed feeling more depressed and inadequate as I failed my children by not being available for them and failed my husband by not being able to maintain an uncomplicated pregnancy.

As the Christmas season approached, I finally reached full-term status. I was due in the winter, however as with most women at the last stages of pregnancy, any day would do.

My obstetrician finally paroled me from bed rest on Christmas Eve and I was able to celebrate the holidays with family, hugely pregnant and hugely uncomfortable. I was unquestionably very large. Since being restricted to bed, I had gained more than 70 pounds! Of course, this didn't stop me from celebrating Christmas Eve with extended family as I piled my dinner plate high with ham and mashed potatoes, the traditional Christmas Eve meal in our family.

Christmas Eve celebration was healing for me. I once again felt vital to my family and remained hopeful that our pregnancy was reaching a point where fear of loss was no longer consuming my consciousness.

David and I returned home with the children around 11 p.m. and hurried them off to bed as they awaited the arrival of Santa Claus the following morning. Within three hours of a sound sleep, I awoke to the sharpest most dreadful stomach pains I could recall.

"Oh shit!" I thought as I woefully remembered what was happening and prepared myself for what was to come. Each cramp, each contraction came with a fury. Relentless, rhythmic waves started from zero to sixty in less than two minutes.

All I could chant, all I could think was the mantra of women in labor the world over, "Why did I do this again?"

I hurriedly showered and blew my hair dry as the contractions intensified. The pressure in my vagina tripled and I could feel the baby dropping centimeter by centimeter in search of the exit. Still, I was determined to put on my make-up before heading to the hospital. Worst case scenario: I would deliver my child at home. I could do it. After all, I am a nurse.

After dressing and becoming more presentable, my next task was to wake the children and let them know the baby was going to arrive soon. This task brought much more challenge and frustration than I had anticipated. As the hour neared 3 a.m., my two young children awoke with the belief that Santa had just arrived. They never expected to hear that Christmas needed to wait a while because mommy and daddy were going to the hospital to have a baby. The excitement that these two young children were soon going to have a new baby brother or sister was strongly foreshadowed by the realization that Christmas was going to be postponed.

With that news, my two loveable children became instantly consumed with sadness, their eyes flooded with tears. In an attempt to diffuse this chaos, I began a mad frenzy of shaking wrapped Christmas gifts under the tree so that I could bring gifts to the hospital for them to open later in the day. I huffed and groaned and rocked through contractions in search of the treasures under the tree that might remedy the sadness of a Christmas tainted by the birth of a sibling. As soon as I bundled up a few gifts, we were off to the hospital.

Less than 90 minutes after our arrival at the hospital, Danny was born: eight pounds, 21 inches long. As I rested, recovered, and once again thanked God for this amazing blessing I couldn't help but wonder how could he weigh only eight pounds when I gained seventy? How was this possible?

CHAPTER 13

Controlled Chaos
at Home

*L*ife was hectic after Danny's birth. I recovered from his delivery for a few weeks and then prepared to finish my baccalaureate studies. My professors and classmates were completely supportive during my pregnancy and recovery. I became a real-life case study that could be analyzed in the classroom. Time flew by and I graduated in the fall, just a few months behind my classmates. That was pretty amazing since I had lost so much study time during my pregnancy.

I secured my dream job on the labor and delivery floor of a nearby hospital. I struggled to balance work and my personal life. When I woke up each morning and transformed myself with hairspray and make-up, I was putting on my mask. I went to work wearing normal on my face, but never feeling it in my soul. I was different. My childhood was different. My family life was different. But work was healing me. My success as a nurse made me feel more normal. Each woman who thanked me for my support as she struggled with her own birth empowered me and helped heal my ego. Work became my priority, to the detriment of my family.

David became the primary caregiver for our three children and housekeeper as well as working full-time himself. I worked constantly. I would work holidays and overtime to supplement our household income not comprehending the considerable stress it was causing on my marriage.

I didn't realize the load I was placing on David's shoulders at the time because I was so consumed with a job that was completely satisfying to me on many levels. I enjoyed my work and looked forward every day to providing care for women with the added bonus of watching babies being born.

My career provided me sanctuary from all the pain of my past experience. My work became my road toward self-healing as I was increasingly able to see myself as a mentor to women in my community and an example of the ability to overcome life's challenges.

What I was unable to see during these years was that, as my success grew, I was becoming more ego-driven and arrogant at home. This behavior challenged my marriage and in my unending search for success, I began to drive David away.

I would like to say that I didn't realize this was happening, but this would not be entirely true. In reality, I did understand that I was becoming more challenging for him to be around and I didn't care enough at the time to change my behavior.

I was more successful and more independent than I had ever been before. With this new-found success, I was consumed with being and doing whatever I wanted to do regardless of how my spouse might feel about my choices. I was becoming selfish. Additionally, as my success grew, so did interest from male colleagues. So, a combination of my own ego and admiring attention from other men really created a time in my marriage where David was not very high on my priority list. Therefore, our marriage was nearly lost.

Six years after Danny's birth, the stress of my career continued to wear down my marriage and was also starting to wear me down physically. I had worked tirelessly through those years, hoping to build a good reputation with my leaders with the hope of personal advancement.

In my small community, a new doctor arrived with his family after he completed his residency. Roger seemed friendly and with a wife and children close in age to my older children, we became amicable quickly and I enjoyed spending time with him on the labor floor. He made me laugh.

Several months passed and Roger pronounced his physical attraction to me. I naively failed to realize this might cause conflict in the workplace. I was at a weak time in my marriage when Roger first told me he was attracted to me. David and I were fighting constantly and had several conversations about divorce. Roger's interest in me was an unfortunate, but welcome distraction from my unhappy life. I wasn't interested in him, but the attention felt good.

The rough patch in my marriage lasted for more than a year and I honestly can say that there were times when I didn't want to try anymore. During that time, I felt misunderstood and mistreated and I thought David did not understand my feelings or all the challenges I was going through.

In hindsight, I can say with certainty that I have a great deal of responsibility for David's detachment. However at the time, I was far too angry and hostile to consider that possibility.

Roger was a safe substitute for me. He provided compliments and simple attention, plus he was married, too. I translated this attention into a fantasy man like Roger who would care about me without judgment. I was never physically attracted to Roger and I think this was what made him appear to be safe to me. I had no desire to begin a sexual relationship with him, but I liked the flirtation.

My loneliness at home enhanced my enjoyment of Roger's attention, even though I knew it was wrong. Roger became a temporary substitute for emotional intimacy during the time

David and I were devoid of passion. Simple compliments and knowing that another man found me desirable was dangerous in a marriage where I felt unwanted.

This brief moment in time lasted only a few months and ended quite abruptly when I had one of my many "light-bulb" moments during a conversation with Brandon, who was seeking relationship advice from his mother, a person with whom he placed trust. At that moment, I realized that I had no business offering advice to my son if I was perpetuating lies in my own relationship.

I recognized that any form of attention from another man really was infidelity. I knew I didn't want to be untrue to David. I needed to decide if my marriage was salvageable or if it was time for David and me to part ways. Regardless of my decision, Roger was never a part of my plans for the future nor was I in his. I shared these feelings with Roger the next time we spoke. He seemed to accept my decision and I interpreted this as sincere.

My marriage was still unraveling at home, but I couldn't avoid the inevitable conversation with David to determine where our marriage was heading.

One evening when I returned home from work, I asked David if we could speak. I dumped all of my unhappiness, frustration and anger in an emotionally fueled monologue that lasted most of the night. David did the same. We yelled, we cried and we almost threw in the towel more than once, but in the end we chose as a team to make the necessary changes to improve our marriage and to be better people.

Roger and I worked together with a lapse in flirtation as he pursued another nurse. My marriage began to improve, but my mask remained.

CHAPTER 14

Chaos at Work

I had worked with Roger for over a year before my relationship with him became bizarre. In that time, David and I had begun the welcome healing of our marriage and we devoted specific days each week to either private "date" nights or "family" nights as our way to balance both important components of our lives.

As my marriage improved, Roger's marriage deteriorated. In the beginning, I did not think too much about it, but in retrospect, by the end of our working relationship, I was able to see there was a line crossed at that time. My relationship with Roger transformed from a professional one to a pattern of sexual harassment.

The first sign that my working relationship with Roger was changing came when I returned from a long weekend in Philadelphia with David.

In the weeks before, Roger had begun to exhibit subtle signs suggesting he was jealous of my husband and the time I spent with him. Roger began discouraging me from going home after my shift ended, asking me to stay at the hospital and spend time talking with him. Roger also began to make inappropriate comments about phone conversations he overheard me having with David, cementing my suspicion he was jealous.

Over time, the inappropriate behavior expanded outside of the hospital where we worked. Our children attended the same school and it was inevitable that we would see each other at school performances or sporting events. When Roger was unaccompanied by his wife, he would frequently comment to me about "how hot I looked in those jeans" or similar sexually suggestive remarks. I began to feel suffocated in a role that went far beyond that of a professional colleague. Initially, I brushed off Roger's comments, aware that he was unhappy in his personal life. He constantly complained about his wife and her ineptness. But, by the time David and I went on our get-away, I began to see more clearly the underlying issue that was bothering Roger.

When I shared stories with Roger about all the fun we had during that fantastic weekend, Roger's demeanor abruptly shifted. The best I can describe it is he suddenly transformed into a jealous boyfriend.

I pointed out to him that he was acting jealous. He paused for several seconds before admitting that he supposed he was jealous.

I was stunned by his comment. I thought, "Oh shit, this isn't good."

I replayed his recent change in behavior over and over again in my mind. What was I supposed to do? Roger and I worked together frequently and he had admitted being jealous of my relationship with my husband. In my mind, I again downplayed his feelings and chalked them off to his unhappiness with his wife. I convinced myself this event was really nothing serious and no further action was necessary.

Roger and I carried on with our work that day with nothing more said. I became careful to avoid sharing personal stories with Roger that might create further jealous feelings. I rationalized that even if Roger was jealous, those feelings would likely pass once he really began to see that being involved with me was no bargain.

In my mind, I was a screw up. I wasn't normal, therefore he would eventually see that his jealousy was misplaced. Let's face it, I have a more scandalous past than most women and so I rationalized that any infatuation he might feel was likely going to resolve itself.

Work continued and seasons passed, but Roger's infatuation was undiminished. I had learned early in that period that if I gave Roger the attention he wanted, it made a significant difference in good work days verses bad ones. Roger wanted attention from me that made him feel special. If I failed to give him the attention he expected, he would become irritable or pout, whining that I didn't like him anymore.

Greeting him with a daily hug and kiss when no other colleagues were nearby kept him content for a while. He never pressured me for more intimate sexual contact, but he had an expectation of frequent physical contact with me when we were alone. Occasionally, he would squeeze my bottom. The sexual comments were endless.

I felt trapped. I was working with a man who required me to fill a void in his personal life. I couldn't avoid him in the job I currently had. This was the job I worked so hard for, the job that made me so passionately happy. I saw no option but to endure.

Brandon would soon be going to college and David and I were both working hard to prepare for retirement. So, I bargained with myself and rationalized that a few hugs and kisses were okay given the alternative of losing a job that I loved and an income my family depended on.

In addition to my stress at work, which I shared with no one, David and I were being challenged by some significant emotional and behavioral problems with Brandon. I was being torn apart at home with a difficult child and reduced to nurse toy at work with a physician who couldn't shake his infatuation for me. Life really sucked, again.

CHAPTER 15

Anxiety Disorder Challenges my Son

During the summer Brandon graduated from high school and before his departure for college, I received a telephone call that changed our family dynamic in a profound way.

It was Mary, the mother of Brandon's girlfriend, Anne. Anne had recently broken up with him. Mary said she had some serious concerns about Brandon and needed to speak with me urgently.

I agreed and we met within a few hours. She said Brandon was acting inappropriately and that she was very concerned about his safety. My heart sank. Adrenaline surged through my body and my chest began to ache, but I fought for composure, trying to control any expression of anxiety that might become apparent through my facial expression or outward physical tremors.

Mary said she had reason to believe that Brandon was cutting himself and threatening to cause himself harm as a result of the break-up with Anne.

I sat paralyzed as I listened to the words, trying to process those actions in relationship to my child.

All I could utter was, "What?" and Mary repeated the story.

I had just spent the morning with Brandon in a joint therapy session, sitting to his immediate right. There was no mention of him causing harm to himself, nor did I see any marks that appeared suspicious. The only logical explanation was that perhaps Brandon was making up this story to make Anne feel guilty for their break-up and was trying to manipulate her emotions. I had no reason to believe he would actually harm himself, however I would consider he would try to create a drama for attention from Anne. We spoke a while longer and I expressed my thanks for her sincere concern, agreeing to let her know the outcome.

I returned home to find Brandon watching television and appearing to be without any concern at the moment.

"Let me see your wrists," I demanded, interrupting his entertainment.

"What? Why?" he asked in a surprised voice, attempting to avoid my request.

"You heard me," I said firmly, my anxiety quickly mixing with anger. I had just received information from a woman I barely knew that my son was harming himself.

Brandon pulled up the long sleeves of his sweatshirt. There on each wrist were fresh wounds pink and raised, superficial but definitely self-inflicted. Residual blood remained on one wrist, probably from earlier that morning. The others appeared to be a week or so old.

"Dear, God, IT IS TRUE!" I thought. "My son is cutting himself. What the hell is next?"

After I inspected his arms and the rest of his body, we had a long conversation about Brandon's state of mind. I told him I was floored that I could sit next to my son in a therapist's office while he pretended to be okay, when actually he was harming himself without my knowledge. He was nearly 18 years old and, in my eyes, his future looked fabulous. So, why in the world would he cause harm to himself? All the possibilities swirled through my mind, including the potential that he suffered from a mental illness like my mother.

My son was struggling and my familiar pattern began to run in my mind again: It was because I was a failure as a mother.

Brandon had always been my most challenging child. He was hyper-reactive as a toddler and never learned that "no" means "no." He threw endless temper tantrums in his quest to get his own way. He was a head banger and in early childhood, he often had a large bruised knot on his forehead that was the symbol of demanding his own way. His siblings were more calm easygoing kids; Brandon was the strong-willed stubborn one. With Brandon, I always had to be alert for his sneakiness and deception. He gave David and me a challenge in his quest to always "get one over" on his parents.

Brandon looked for loopholes when we gave him instructions that he didn't agree with. Here's a funny example that David and I frequently recall: One night we were heading out to dinner and the children were being cared for by my father, "Grandpa" to his grandchildren. They were given strict instructions that the kitchen was closed with the exception of fruit if they became hungry. They had finished dinner and if they wanted a snack we had grapes, bananas, and other fruit from which they could choose.

Celeste was fine with this and Brandon appeared fine, but no sooner did we leave, Brandon made the executive decision that Skittles candy would be an acceptable fruit substitute. When David and I returned home to learn that Skittles were the snack Brandon had chosen, his rationale was, "Well I thought they would be okay because they are fruit flavored." Brandon found his loophole and ran with it.

This is pretty much the story of his childhood. As he grew, the challenges for us as his parents grew as well. Of course, I loved him and I persevered, praying daily that he would grow out of this behavior. Brandon was evaluated by his pediatrician and never viewed as anything other than a hyper-reactive child.

No, he wasn't hyperactive. The diagnosis was hyper-reactive which is different. Brandon was a great kid when all was going according to his plan, but when he had to shift gears and follow a path he didn't like, he would react in an inappropriate manner. I was encouraged to read books about the variety of personality types of children and to learn how to cope with his behavior. He never needed medications. As a matter of fact, he was a very good student and got along well in the classroom. This supported the diagnosis that I later learned was simple manipulative behavior, very much like my mother exhibited throughout most of my life.

By the time I learned about his self-destructive behavior, Brandon had been accepted to four of the five colleges to which he had applied and would be leaving home in a few short months. I had little time to help a son who was obviously experiencing something seriously wrong. I had no experience with cutting and other self-destructive behavior; my best plan to cope was to begin intensive therapy right away as a family and individually. I needed to understand why he was behaving this way, so therapy seemed the best plan.

I tried my best to understand what was going through his mind and what our family could do to deal with this crisis. We spent several days a week in therapy either individually and as a family, listening and speaking and crying, desperately trying to understand why and how to make Brandon better. We might as well have moved into the therapist's office that summer, because it seemed that we spent more time there than at home. But David and I were committed to helping Brandon overcome this destructive behavior as his departure for college quickly approached.

My gut told me that Brandon was not ready to leave home

and be out of his family environment. I was worried that sending him off in that frame of mind could lead to disastrous consequences. Deep in my spirit, I was terrified he would try to kill himself. As mid-August approached, I told the therapist I thought Brandon was not yet ready to leave home. The therapist disagreed.

"Brandon needs to leave home and begin a fresh start away from his ex-girlfriend so he can heal," he said. "I understand your concerns, but they are unwarranted at this time. Brandon needs to get away and see if he can shake off his behavior."

I debated this question for a few weeks. The pediatrician started him on a low dose anti-depressant just two weeks before transition to his college, a four-hour drive from home. I watched and waited, seeking signs of improvement, anything at all to suggest that Brandon was in recovery phase. The best I could see he was not harming himself and it appeared he was looking forward to a new environment and all the change involved with college life. Maybe the therapist was right. Change could foster healing. So September came and Brandon was off to college. All we could do was hope for the best.

CHAPTER 16

Trying to Save My Family

*I*t was a nightmare for me with Brandon being away from home. I don't think I slept two consecutive nights that fall, his freshman semester. He was four hours from home and we spoke daily, but he was in a very bizarre emotional place and seemed to be unable to move out of his negative behavior.

Most of the time, he seemed detached and distant. I was very fearful that he was still harming himself and really had no way of assessing him when he was not living in our home. Brandon claimed he was taking his anti-depressants as prescribed, but within a few weeks, his behavior spiraled out of control.

I was at work one day when I called Brandon to check on him. He started the conversation speaking very erratically about Anne and her family and was even suggesting that he was going to cause them harm. I frantically tried to process his words and determine if this was detached anger or a seemingly sincere statement and a legitimate warning of his intent to harm them.

As Brandon continued to speak rapidly, barely taking a breath, he sounded more and more erratic and unstable. All I could think was, "Oh dear God, what do I do? What do I do?"

I scrambled in my mind to develop a plan to manage this

child and figure out why he was falling apart. When he finally completed his monologue filled with rage toward Anne's family, I begged him to stay put in his room and told him I was coming to visit him just as soon as I finished my shift at work. My job was actually an hour closer to him than my home, so it wouldn't take as long.

He agreed he wouldn't go anywhere, so I rushed to finish my work day and get to my son, who was obviously falling apart. I also called David and asked him to speak with Brandon and do his own assessment of Brandon's state of mind. I hoped that perhaps I was just over-exaggerating and my son wasn't so bad after all. I tried to hold on to a glimmer of hope that maybe I was just overreacting and David would reassure me that Brandon was just fine.

No such luck this time. David agreed that Brandon appeared to be seriously irrational and that he needed immediate help. We decided to phone the college's emergency hotline that was intended to address issues such as this, and advise them of the situation and that I was en route.

The people working the hotline were very patient and reassuring. By the time I had reached Brandon's dorm room they were already there, speaking with him along with the local police who were called for assistance.

I could see at the first glance that Brandon was in a seriously bad frame of mind and we all agreed he needed a prompt psychiatric evaluation. Brandon's eyes were dark and hollow. His expression was empty, detached and devoid of emotion. I could see my son losing reality right before my eyes while I stood helpless and fearful.

Eight hours later, an evaluation by a team of mental health experts provided some answers to Brandon's behavior. The most encouraging of the news was that Brandon was extremely unlikely to harm anyone. The experts decided that Brandon's rant about harming Anne or her family was nothing more than a young man with an attitude problem who wasn't able to manipulate people and get his own way.

We knew from the summer's counseling sessions that Brandon was hurting because of the breakup and, because he felt pain, he was in turn trying to cause Anne and her family pain by making false threats.

In a nutshell, he wasn't getting his own way, so he was escalating his manipulation to a level that he thought would bring Anne back to him. Unfortunately, he was unable to recognize the consequences were going to be much more harmful to him and he didn't recognize that manipulation rarely got the results he was seeking. This was pretty much Brandon's theme during his childhood. He was a great kid when things went his way and impossible to deal with when they didn't.

I was completely exhausted, both physically and mentally. As dawn neared after a night of sitting in the waiting room of a psychiatric facility dreading a diagnosis of doom, I could not accept that my son was manipulating and that this behavior was calculated.

"Are you sure he is not bipolar or schizophrenic?" I asked. There had to be a more organic cause of why someone would behave so erratically and with such detached manner.

"No, Ms. Maat, your son is a troubled young man who needs to accept that life isn't always going to go the direction he expects it should," the doctors told me.

At dawn, Brandon was released to my care, still taking the same anti-depressant and under the advice that he needed to begin weekly therapy to learn better coping skills. Certainly, this was a much better diagnosis than a mental illness, but I was still questioning how my child could behave in such an extreme manner simply because he wasn't getting what he wanted.

I drove Brandon home and we all spent the weekend recovering from fatigue. I just wanted to decompress, understand why this was happening, and most importantly, to make it stop.

I was very fortunate to reach out to Dr. Z., a local psychiatrist, who was willing to meet with Brandon on a weekly basis and provide guidance to all of us. Brandon began weekly visits with Dr. Z. as he resumed college the following Monday. He took a three hour-long bus ride each way to his weekly appointment with the doctor. David and I struggled throughout the semester allowing Brandon to remain at school, but the professionals believed that was the best plan for the moment.

My new "normal" became weekly long-distance visits to my son. I picked him up at the bus station to bring to and from his psychiatrist appointments. I tried to appear pleasant at work each day. I maintained my role of wife and mother at home to the other two children who didn't understand this madness.

Unfortunately, my other children suffered the most. Although I was able to muddle through work, I really had no energy reserve by the time I got home. By the early winter, I was juggling the family challenge of a very troubled son while trying to balance my family life as a wife and mother to my other children, who were experiencing the consequences of their brother's instability.

In addition, I was being more and more challenged by Roger. I tried to find ways to avoid working directly with him by asking other nurse colleagues to exchange patient assignments with me without drawing attention to my situation. On the labor floor with so many curious people, I had no doubt it would not take long for that attention to come.

Roger appeared pleasant in front of others; however he would seek out private time with me where he would behave more flirtatiously as he continued his ridiculous and unwanted pursuit. His relentless behavior was making it impossible for me to function professionally. Almost like a jealous suitor, he demanded my personal attention, including hugs and flirtatious behavior whenever he could get me alone.

I was trapped. My obligation to my children required all I could give as a mother to help Brandon through his crisis and provide stability to the best of my ability for Celeste and Danny.

At the same time, I was under enormous pressure to be a play toy for a physician who was very well respected in our community. Roger tried to fill the void of an unhappy home life with this workplace flirtation that had become an obsession.

I had no refuge. I had no space and no opportunity to escape from the daily pressure of my life to take care of myself and my own needs. Quite frankly, during that time, I did not even have the time to recognize that I had needs. I was consumed by stress, fear, guilt and several other unnamed emotions that affect a mother challenged by an emotionally unhealthy child. I was entirely consumed with my efforts to help Brandon heal and protect my other children. Somehow, unbelievably, it never occurred to me to turn to David for solace.

Something had to give, so at work it was just easiest to give Roger what he wanted. I once again became an actress. I put on a mask and I pretended by giving the empty hugs and empty flirtation that he expected while at work. I had no energy left to try to resolve that issue. In fact, I knew in my inner being, in my core, I couldn't resolve it. He was a physician. I was just a nurse. His job was more valuable than mine and given a choice, I was the expendable one. Roger wanted my attention and I needed my job, even more so in a time of family crisis.

During that time, I was very much like the actress I had become the afternoon so many years ago when I engaged in that humiliating sexual act as a means to win the return of my absconded child, my baby Brandon.

There I was, nearly twenty years later, pretending to be something I wasn't in order to secure my position within a workplace that held me at its mercy. I needed my income and was in no position to give it up. A nurse reporting inappropriate behavior by a physician was the kiss of death. I would most definitely lose my job one way or another, and would very likely not find another one in my small community.

So, in my mind, I justified my behavior and told myself it was okay. I hugged Roger every time he wanted it, in a desperate effort to make my work life more tolerable. That attention seemed to keep him satisfied for a while, so I played the role. During my drive from home to work every day, I'd have to psyche myself up to assume my role as the "other me," the "nurse toy." David and the rest of my family had no idea of my dual life.

I tried to detach from my home stress and prepare for my day at the hospital where, if Roger was not working, it would be a good day. If he was working, I would do what it took to keep him happy just for a little peace. At the time, it seemed a small price to pay for the salary that my family needed as we became more and more challenged by medical bills. I was wife, mother, nurse and actress. Perhaps actress was my first role.

Looking back, this was a dark time in my life. Everything I thought I had overcome seemed to be flooding back into my new existence. I felt like I was drowning. I recall growing up and thinking about how I was going to be a better mother than my mother was. I was going to be the best wife I could be, and I was going to be the best nurse. I needed to be everything I thought I was supposed to be. Yet, everything I was supposed to be, everything I was striving to become, was being challenged by obstacles that I could not overcome. I was failing as a mother, as a wife and as a nurse, therefore I was failing myself. I couldn't understand what the purpose of being was and even came to a point of questioning God's existence.

I felt empty. I was devoid of faith and desperately hanging on through the only survival skill that worked for me, manipulation. Funny, that is what Brandon did, too. I wonder where he learned that . . . ??

It was through my inherent survival skill of manipulation that I was trying to make the best of my work situation. I was once again the "actress" playing the role of making a man in my life happy by giving him the attention he demanded. I was leaving work only to return home and be the "actress" to my husband and children. I pretended that work went well and life was good as I desperately strove to create a family life that portrayed some sense of normalcy. I was actress to the patients, giving truly sound advice to each woman encouraging, empowering and lifting them up to be strong, healthy and happy individuals. I was supporting them in labor as they worked hard to become mothers while I questioned my own maternal abilities so deeply.

It was all a lie. I was living a lie, trying to hang on to my dream of normalcy that I wanted so desperately to come to fruition. In the end though, the act became so confusing and convoluted that even I couldn't discern what truth was. I was becoming the lie.

CHAPTER 17

A Whirlwind
of Darkness

*B*randon's first semester at college ended in December with a renewed crisis in our home when we announced to him that he would not be returning to college the following semester. When his grades arrived by mail, my son's high school average of 3.4 had evaporated to a 1.7. He simply wasn't emotionally ready for this level of independence.

By that time, the experts finally agreed. Brandon needed to be home to work on his emotional healing and either postpone college for a bit, or attend community college nearby. That decision was entirely up to him, but college away from home was no longer an option. I recall Celeste learning about Brandon's astonishing drop in his G.P.A. as she smugly told her brother, "What the hell? The dog could have done better." The bottom line was Brandon needed to take care of himself first. School could come later.

The news caused fireworks in our home. I mean fireworks! Brandon quite literally went berserk when he was told that he needed to focus on his emotional healing and that he could enroll in community college if he chose. His response to our decision involved throwing kitchen chairs, making threats, punching holes in the hallway wall and other violent acts with no regard for his siblings' presence.

The family endured a living hell for nearly six weeks. Brandon's anger erupted nearly every day.

True to form, Brandon was not prepared to take "no" for an answer and he was willing to push it to the limit to get his own way. In the late winter, Brandon walked up the stairs with a knife and superficially cut his wrists in front of me and Danny, who was then eight years old.

What could prompt so much rage in my son? That particular day, his rage at our refusal to allow him to return to school was coupled with our refusal to allow him to use the car that evening to drive an hour to a party at a friend's house.

The police and ambulance arrived at our home and after being evaluated in the local emergency room of the hospital where I worked; Brandon was involuntarily committed to an in-patient psychiatric facility for a week. His irrational behavior had escalated to a level that placed him in the care of the state. He was then committed as an in-patient until he was deemed safe to leave.

The few weeks between Brandon leaving school and his residence in the psychiatric facility had been a nightmare for all of us. We stood our ground with our son, remaining firm in our decision that he was not returning to college under any circumstances. This firm stand really pre-empted the excessively irrational, manipulative behavior of my son as he considered his options and chose to push the envelope and show us just how far he would go to get his own way. His behavior landed him a week in a locked facility and the unfortunate scars on his wrists that even time can't heal.

In all honesty, while Brandon was in the psychiatric ward, I got the best sleep I had in months. Finally, my son was in a controlled environment and under the supervision of mental health professionals. David and I had gotten into the habit of sleeping with one eye open each night, fearing Brandon's instability and the violence we knew he might commit. We were afraid of our son in our own home.

"Your son has an attitude problem," Dr. Z told us, standing firmly by his diagnosis that Brandon was not mentally challenged or mentally ill.

"He doesn't like what he hears and he is willing to do whatever it takes to get his own way," Dr. Z added.

Brandon had escalated his battle to return to college by causing harm to himself. He was clearly telling us that he would do anything to get his way, even harm himself.

However, his self-mutilation was very calculated. He was precise in his location and the superficiality of the injuries he inflicted on himself. He knew that he was choosing places for his cuts that were less likely to be fatal or cause permanent damage.

This was little consolation to me, knowing how far my son was willing to go to get his own way in an argument. Dare I say it was no consolation at all?

But the diagnosis remained consistent with all the mental health professionals who saw him, and their treatment recommendations did not change. They advised David and me to remain steadfast in our decisions and not show Brandon any sign that we were waffling or unsure.

Brandon would take any perception of our uncertainty as his personal sign to push us further for his own way, we were told. Further, Dr. Z. and his colleagues said that Brandon needed to learn that "no" meant "NO," whether he liked it or not.

In his childhood and his adolescence, we didn't teach Brandon that lesson well enough, so we were suffering the consequences. Somehow, Brandon learned that "no" sometimes meant "maybe." If he pushed us hard enough, we sometimes gave up the fight with him and eventually said "yes." Therefore, in his mind, the fight was worth it because sometimes he did prevail.

Brandon was discharged after one week in the mental health facility with an order of protection for us granted by the local family court. This order of protection allowed Brandon to return to our home with the strictest of conditions that he was forbidden any acts of violence in our home.

It was humiliating for me to have to return to the same family court judge who had helped return Brandon to me 17 years earlier after my son was abducted by his father.

My goal was to scare my son straight. I brought him before the judge and briefly explained the violent acts that Brandon had committed in our home and asked the judge for any assistance that he could give. Judge H. spoke firmly to Brandon and told him in no uncertain terms there would be, "No more violent behavior!"

Judge H. explained the consequences to Brandon who was then 18 years old and considered an adult in our state. If he got into trouble, he would be tried as an adult. Brandon seemed to understand.

CHAPTER 18

Time for Me/ Time of Shame

I turned 40 that same year, just a few months before the struggles with my son and at the same time my situation with Roger at work was escalating. In my mind, David and I were doing well financially despite the mounting medical bills for my son. Our investments were growing and I desperately needed some personal luxury. For the first time in my life, I felt financially secure; a feeling I had never before experienced.

David grew up in a middle class family far removed from the struggles that I had experienced. When we met, he was already well established in his accounting career and his success was completely due to his own motivation and discipline. It was really the start of that year when I began to be able to enjoy more indulgences, things that I had only dreamed of like great vacations and nice cars. So, with the start of my fourth decade, I began to make plans to indulge myself in a few things I desired.

One evening at work as I went into the nurse's locker room to get something out of my handbag, I found a plastic bag in the back of my locker that I hadn't placed there. I wasn't sure how the unfamiliar bag got there or what was in it. My locker had no private lock on it. None of us locked our lockers. My nurse colleagues and I had worked together for years and we were all friends as well as co-workers. To place a lock on my locker would have implied my lack of trust in my friends. I casually opened it to see what was inside and was stunned to find a stack of pornographic material.

"What the F***?" was all that went through my mind. I had absolutely no understanding how this had gotten into my locker. I became very frightened. Despite the fear that ate at my gut, my inner voice said that Roger had to be behind this in some way. He was the only person I could deduce would be involved.

Later, when Roger and I were alone, I closed the door to the room and asked him if he had placed this material in my locker.

He hesitated for a moment and acted surprised despite his obvious intention for me to find what he had planted in my personal space, just so that he could interpret my reaction. His response suggested that the bag had been there for quite a while before I noticed it. That scared me even more. I asked why he would do something like that. In no uncertain terms, I demanded that he remove the bag immediately.

I was furious and enraged, but looking back, I realize now that I felt violated. Someone I trusted and thought was my colleague and had been a friend had placed me in a dangerous legal position. He put pornography in my workspace and subjected me to what could be immediate dismissal. When asked why, he just smirked and said he was hoping I would agree to watch it with him one night. My mind was spinning! My life was crumbling! It was an escalation of Roger's violation of my person and my space.

Despite my insistence that Roger remove that bag from my private space, several days passed before he actually removed it. After about a week, it was finally gone.

Some people may ask why I didn't promptly report this to my superiors. This is certainly a fair and reasonable question.

The best answer I can offer is that he is a physician and I am not. In my community, he would be protected. If I had reported him, it would be the end of *my* career, not his. I was painfully aware of this.

I didn't report him and I continue to live with the knowledge that I failed to protect myself. I knew what he had done was wrong, but I swept it under the rug because I needed and wanted my job.

After the porn was removed from my locker, I dropped the subject and carried on with my work responsibilities. But the fear of Roger remained with me from that moment forward. In addition, the unhappier life became for Roger at home with his wife, the more pressure was added on me to fill that void for him. His infatuation with me seemed to grow despite his clear understanding that David and I were doing well. It had become an obsession.

In hindsight, I think the porn served as a not-so-subtle threat. It made me even more afraid of Roger and more fearful that I could so easily lose my job when I was finally finding some security.

That spring, I reached a decision to undergo cosmetic surgery and planned to take a few weeks of vacation time for my recovery. After breastfeeding three children, my breasts needed a lift. I consulted a plastic surgeon colleague. For the record, let me say that I am a firm believer in people's choice to enhance or modify their bodies. This includes piercings, tattoos and cosmetic surgery. If the person is informed and weighs the risks and benefits, then that choice should be respected without judgment.

I scheduled a breast procedure and used my vacation time for recovery, not medical leave. Unfortunately, my healing time was interrupted with repeated phone calls from Roger, who knew why I had taken time off work. He would never leave a voice message; he would just continue to call over the course of a day until I finally answered the phone. When I finally did pick up, he would reprimand me for taking so long to speak with him and complain that I was ignoring him and being inconsiderate. For whatever reason, Roger was unable to see that I was healing and did not want to be disturbed.

David recognized this pattern as well. He made comments once in a while, but basically he just let it go.

When I returned to work, I wore a special surgical bra necessary for healing. I was well enough that I could return to administrative work on the labor floor, but could not assist with actual patient care. Regardless, I was happy to get back to being busy.

The first day back, Roger greeted me and instructed me to meet him in the physician locker room, "Come in and close the door." I naturally did what I was instructed to do without questioning his reason.

"Well, let's see them," he demanded.

I hesitated, shocked and stunned. I stalled for time, explaining that I had bandages on and that there was really nothing to see. He remained firm in his demand. I knew Roger and I knew he would not take "no" for answer; interestingly, much like my eldest son.

Rather than face his anger, it was just easier to comply. Filled with shame for not standing my ground and protecting myself, I opened my shirt, opened my surgical bra, and let him stare at my bandaged, bruised, and healing breasts. He soaked in the image without comment.

After a few moments, I re-hooked my bra, closed my shirt and left for the bathroom before continuing my work day. I closed the bathroom door for a moment of privacy to wipe the tears of humiliation from my eyes.

CHAPTER 19

The Tipping Point

I am fortunate to love my job and I am eager to get out of bed every morning to go to work. At least up that point, I was fortunate. Oh yes, there were those cold winter days where climbing out of warm blankets was the absolute last thing I wanted to do, but nevertheless, I always loved my job.

I am a nurse. All I ever wanted to be was a nurse. My calling is to care for women, to help in childbirth and to empower women on their life journeys. Overcoming childhood adversity and obstacles in my personal life left me with a feeling that I was well suited to counsel other women on their paths. With this philosophy, I enjoyed my career. Unfortunately, with Roger's arrival in my community, my life began to unravel.

Roger's behavior became more erratic and inappropriate during that winter.

My workplace was increasingly becoming a prison for me rather than a medical healing environment. The more Roger reported being unhappy at home, the more he expected me to fill that void. Secret hugs and kisses shared during work hours. He seemed to love the forbidden thrill that came with almost being caught by others. I just wanted to die.

I was trapped.

Every time I tried to avoid his leer or his touch, he became offended and gave me not-so-subtle signals of his disapproval. My one-time dream job had turned into a prison. I watched the clock as each patient came in and came out. By the end of my work day, I would grab my car keys and plan my hasty exit. Years passed as I tried to make the best of a bad situation. I never realized how much I was enduring until the nightmare finally reached its climax. My failure to recognize the seriousness of my situation distresses me almost as much as the horror story that was unfolding day by day.

I knew that I was struggling. I knew things weren't right, but I kept convincing myself that I could work it out. I believed that Roger's attraction was destined to fizzle out and that he would eventually leave me alone. I believed that if I ignored him long enough, he would finally get the message. I continued justifying the bad situation in so many ways.

Throughout the interminable legal process that was to follow, I was often asked, "Why?"

Why didn't I quit my job? Why didn't I report Roger? Why didn't I do a thousand things to stop the pain?

At the time, there was only one answer: I needed my job. I was earning good money and Brandon's treatment and legal expenses were high. I was paying for college. I was paying a mortgage. I was paying for three growing children. I needed my job. Reporting a physician was going to permanently scar my resume. I was never going to find a job like that again in my community. I had a responsibility to my family. So I endured.

I think on another level I somehow believe that I deserved this kind of living hell. It was part of my long-term pattern and the foundation of my mask of normal.

By the following fall, life at work had become unbearable. Once again, the pressure increased the week I returned from a few days off with David. I was rested and in good spirits, ready to get back to business. Roger was not so happy. Within hours of my return to the labor floor, he bombarded me with insults about taking time off to be with my husband.

Initially, I ignored his comments, trying to process why he was in such a foul mood. I never did figure out why he was so upset, but his knowledge that I was away with my husband was very upsetting to him and he wanted me to know it.

Roger started a new tactic: insulting my husband. His new approach was what he thought was flattery: that I had married beneath me and that I deserved better. My head began to spin as I tried to defend myself and my marriage, to no avail. I was furious. He had crossed a line. I knew for certain he was wrong, but I also knew that proving Roger wrong wasn't going to end this fight. He was absolute in his conviction, but I knew that he was really upset because I had been away with David again.

OH DEAR GOD! HOW DID I GET MYSELF INTO THIS POSITION?

The tone of the conversation with Roger escalated as I stood firm, defending myself while fully understanding it was likely making the situation worse. I was so angry that I just didn't care. He wanted my attention. He wanted my time. He wanted me to replace all the unhappiness in his life.

I was sick of it. I wanted my boundaries back. I wanted to stop having to satisfy his need for a relationship. Somehow the boundaries were all blurred. It was time for me to regain control of my body and my role in my workplace. I knew that once I made this decision, in the end it would cost me my job. I didn't care anymore. I had had enough. He had crossed the line that forced my hand.

"F*** him!" I thought, outraged by his gall in passing judgment on my marriage, my family and my choices. How dare he continue to violate my body and my personal space, making it impossible for me to function in a healthy and safe work environment. I was furious.

How did I let this happen? I just did.

Our argument continued for what seemed like hours when suddenly Roger's demeanor changed from hostile and overbearing to one of a pouting small boy. I guess he realized that this argument was pushing me very far away from him. Maybe it was embarrassment or concern that I would report him. Maybe it was because I had finally stood up to him, but his personality shifted and he began to backpedal from the confrontation.

My mind raced at supersonic speed. I was in a tailspin. I immediately realized, "OH, MY GOD! I am right. Think, Amrita. Now what?"

I settled my tone and my posture down to a calm that I didn't feel. I looked at him as if the fight had never happened.

I shrugged my shoulders and left the room.

I returned to the nurse's locker room and closed the bathroom door. My heart was racing, my body shaking as I replayed the events that I had just endured. I looked up to heaven and thought, "This just can't be happening."

But it was.

During that period, it seemed I needed to prove to myself that my theory was correct. Roger liked me too much and I needed to get help with this problem. But how?

I was painfully cautious not to draw my coworkers' attention to myself and Roger. In their eyes, all was status quo and Roger and I were simply friends. I wear a good mask of normal since I have a lifetime of practice. No one would believe that anything unscrupulous was happening behind the scenes.

If I heard this same story from a friend, I could have easily analyzed the situation and advised her that she was being mistreated and even sexually harassed. But I couldn't see it in my own situation. In hindsight, I can now see that I didn't have enough self-worth to recognize the extent of Roger's abuse. I had been emotionally and physically abused all throughout my childhood. I had learned to behave according to the standard of the environment I was in, just to "fit in." Roger wanted me to behave a certain way, so I did. If I made him happy, then work went well. So I just did.

CHAPTER 20

Begging for Help

*S*exual harassment at work is a debilitating problem that for the victim often leads to a no-win situation. In my case, I didn't even identify Roger's inappropriate behavior as sexually harassing. I knew I was being bullied and I knew that he was becoming more and more out of control, but I kept believing that if I persevered I could get control of this situation and make it better.

Being sexually harassed by a person with higher authority is even more problematic because the victim is being mistreated by the very person who is expected to be a mentor. Eventually, the victim becomes worn down physically, emotionally and spiritually.

I was dealing with unbelievable stress at work, so much so that I felt absolute doom each morning I showed up for work. My stomach would burn from anxiety and I would spend my morning drive to work plotting my course of action for the day that would keep me out of Roger's sight as much as possible.

He had grown accustomed to hugs and flirtation and it was becoming more and more difficult to dodge his advances. No matter what I did, it was becoming more and more apparent that my efforts to diffuse Roger's inappropriate behavior were futile.

I changed my routine, switched days off with coworkers, anything I could think of to avoid contact with Roger. I thought this would discourage his advances. However, the more I avoided him, the angrier and more belligerent he became. It became impossible to focus on my work responsibilities and patients who depended upon me for their lives and those of their babies.

Patient care suffered as I became more and more distracted with my attempts to avoid conflict. I felt stalked every time I was on the labor floor and he was there with one of his office patients. I was constantly "on guard." He enjoyed the thrill of the pursuit and the secrecy. I was the target. I was the nurse toy and as such I was expected to put him first on my priority list and to behave in ways that satisfied him. This included sharing meals, hugs, kisses and other secret flirtatious behavior.

Each day that I tried to avoid this contact and reclaim my personal space was a day that I would face private retribution for not complying with his wishes. It was as if I had been unknowingly groomed to meet his needs and when I finally realized this was happening, it was too late to escape. I was trapped.

Each time I avoided physical or emotional contact with him, Roger would behave like a wounded adolescent boy who couldn't get over his crush. I was in a hopeless situation. No matter how I tried to overcome it, I was drowning. As busy as we were with patient care, Roger was still able to remain distracted with me as he maintained this unhealthy need to know my personal business. He was consumed with me in our workplace.

My sense of doom grew as I continued to work in that environment daily, returning home each evening to a household that was still struggling with the challenges of Brandon's emotional crisis.

To add to my profound isolation, I had never once shared

with David what I was experiencing at work. I had no idea how or where to begin trying to share the account of Roger's predatory behavior at work.

In addition, I was afraid. To me, Roger was becoming increasingly irrational in his behavior toward me. He was saying very inappropriate things about his wife that included violence and I was very much in fear for my personal safety. I didn't feel strong enough to share any of this experience with my husband. So, as always, I endured.

By the end of one particular day filled with adolescent jealousy toward my personal time with David, I had reached my limit. The harassment had to end. It was apparent to me in the way he switched off his anger that I was being manipulated very much like the way Brandon behaved.

I couldn't tolerate it any longer. By the afternoon, I summoned the courage to place the call that I knew would likely end my career. I phoned the hospital director and prayed for help as the call connected. I was hoping that this conversation might have a better outcome than I had anticipated. I feared retaliation. Yet I prayed I was wrong.

The conversation was brief, but emotionally charged. I was uncontrollably crying and quite desperate as I requested a meeting as soon as possible to discuss a problem I was having. I was very clear this was not appropriate to speak about over the phone and that I would like to schedule a personal meeting. The secretary assured me she would relay the message to the director and he would be in contact with me. He never called.

Two weeks passed with no return phone call. I knew I was doomed. I continued to endure.

During that time, I learned that I was not the first nurse to complain about Roger. As a matter of fact, as the legal process unfolded years later, I learned the list was longer than I could have imagined. In previous hospitals where he had worked, similar complaints were lodged and none of the women who accused Roger of inappropriate behavior had remained in their jobs.

Yet Roger remained employed. He was a very good obstetrician and was vital to hospital revenue. There is no doubt in my mind that the hospital director learned of the anxiety in my voice in that very brief phone conversation with his secretary. He had no idea the depth of the complaints I planned to share with him. It was this calculated disinterest that assured me that I was doomed. Roger was going to be protected. I was expendable.

I reached deep into my soul to find the resolve to carry on and make the best of a bad situation. The bottom line was unchanged: I needed my income, so I had no choice but to persevere.

Within just a few short weeks, it seemed that the universe was going to take charge and remove me from this unhealthy environment. I didn't have the emotional strength or fortitude to protect myself. Just when it seemed that I would "emotionally snap" one day from the incredible stress at work, I sustained that unforeseen injury where my body "physically snapped" as a way to protect my psyche from any more abuse.

It was in that moment that my injury forcibly removed me from a hostile and abusive work environment. I think somehow my body protected me through this injury when I was unable to protect myself. As strange as it may seem to some, I truly believe that if my elbow didn't shatter that very day, something much worse could have happened to me in the near future. I was being rescued from a situation that I couldn't rescue myself from.

With my broken elbow, I was forced to remove myself from this secretly unhealthy environment and face my circumstances. The overpowering fear I had of Roger during this time was suffocating. The hospital director still had not called me back and I needed to make this desperate situation bearable. The surgery on my elbow proved to be more complex than anticipated and my recovery turned out to be much longer than expected.

I knew I could no longer maintain my sanity if this situation didn't improve. I was becoming more despondent each day. I needed counsel from an outside source. As the weeks passed, I contacted an attorney to guide me through the work-related injury process.

Initially, I spoke to my attorney about my broken elbow and my rights under worker's compensation law. I knew in the back of my mind I wanted to share the darker issue I was experiencing, but I was afraid to speak. Feeling confused and truly helpless, I was terrified to tell somebody my story even though I finally had an opportunity to be heard. Before our meeting ended, I very cautiously mentioned that I had something else I would like to discuss and asked her if she had the time.

I slowly and in great detail shared with her the events of the past few years at work. She listened carefully, interrupting my story once in a while to gain clarity where she felt it was necessary. At the end of my narrative, she diagnosed my case: "Amrita, you are being sexually harassed."

It still amazes me. I live and re-live painful and humiliating events, that until that lawyer's pronouncement, I had never placed a name on my hell in the workplace. I knew Roger's behavior was wrong. I knew it was unacceptable. I knew it was inappropriate, but I had not been able to see it for what it truly was: sexual harassment and intimidation.

A multitude of emotions swept over me as I pondered my lawyer's words. I knew that I was at the end of my rope, that I could no longer be subjected to Roger's increasingly irrational behavior. I had tried to communicate with my hospital's executives about what I was experiencing, but I got a very clear message when they failed to return my calls or to schedule promised meetings. I was desperate for someone to hear me, but no one would listen.

My attorney remained empathetic about my plight, but she clearly spoke of sexual harassment through the lens of the legal system. She warned me that this would not be an easy journey. Sexual harassment victims are often treated like rape victims. I could expect to be accused of "asking for it." I wasn't sure if I had the emotional stamina to proceed.

But before I could consider going any further legally, I needed to share with David what I had been experiencing for the past few years. I had to share the current story, and I had to share the past. David had absolutely no idea what I was experiencing at work.

He and the children would complain that I was coming home irritable and completely unapproachable. Yet, they had no idea the challenges I was experiencing. I blamed myself for this chaos and the fact that the brief emotional relationship from years earlier somehow contributed to my present troubles. I had to share everything with David and release it from my soul. I was holding on to this dark, dirty secret that seemed to be rotting a part of me and contributing to our marital discord.

I prayed for courage as I prepared to share this hidden story with the man I truly loved. I knew I had made a profound mistake, I had made and created a mountainous lie.

David listened. He was angry and I am certain he felt betrayed, although he never specifically told me so. He asked many questions and formulated his own theory. I answered everything honestly and with deep sorrow for the hurt I had caused him and our family. In the end, he forgave me.

I returned to work several weeks later on limited duty as I continued to heal, but I was needed at work to assist my coworkers in an administrative capacity. It took only a week for Roger's sexual flirtation to resume. My anxiety once more became more than I could handle. Work became so unbearable that I was forced to make a decision to either stay and potentially lose my mind, or to leave and bring the issue to the court.

I chose the latter.

I sought personal counsel from Dr. Z. and he advised me to leave work and documented "hostile work environment." With that note, the train of the legal process left the proverbial station. I was setting out for the ride of my life.

The lawsuit began the following winter with the hospital executives assuming no responsibility and ultimately defending the honor of their physician. It took more than a year for depositions to be scheduled. At the depositions, not one of executives ever made eye contact with me. I was the enemy. I think that despite their culpability in my mistreatment by Roger, they hoped I would just go away.

It would unquestionably have been easier for me to just go away, but I couldn't allow them to win. I wanted them to be held accountable for failing to protect me and for allowing a predator to keep working. If I went away, how many other women might suffer the same shame and humiliation? I needed to stand firm and face the people who took away my joy and my happiness. I couldn't give up.

CHAPTER 21

Into Profound Darkness

With the beginning of the legal process came the beginning of the profoundly painful isolation I would endure for the years to come. Coworkers quickly learned that Roger and I were not getting along. They even had theories and personal opinions that they shared with me, but I never shared the depth of my personal experience with them.

Rumors began to fly. A few confided in me that they believed Roger treated me like a wife. They further posited that he was "in love with me and upset because he couldn't have me."

But when it came time for these people to share their opinions in a legal forum, none of these theories re-surfaced. It was no surprise to my co-workers when I left my job. Working with Roger had become unbearable for me, but these women needed to continue to work with him. They knew if they shared the theories they had once shared with me, they could be the next victims.

So I was left on my own to defend myself without anyone else stepping up to speak on my behalf. As the legal process unfolded, hospital staff and executives all seemed to develop amnesia at the same time.

Over the years to follow, as each person was questioned, I

wish I had a dollar for the hundreds, if not thousands, of times I heard very bright, educated people respond to simple questions with, "I don't recall."

Time and time again, any question that offered even the simplest vindication on my behalf was answered by, "I don't recall."

I felt completely sunk. I understood why these people were not speaking truthfully, knowing that they risked retaliation. I wasn't worth it to them. But, the repetitive denial and implicit dishonesty further darkened each day, making it more and more challenging to just breathe.

My attorney told me frankly that I was going to be treated like the "rape victim who deserved it." I kept trying to hold onto the belief that, in the end, people would know that I was telling the truth. I was naïve enough to believe that the truth always prevails.

I got an occasional phone call from former co-workers who would share work news with me and update me on other hospital gossip. Eventually the calls stopped coming and the hospital family with which I spent several years bonding was fading to a memory.

Although I could identify with their dilemma of choosing between Roger and me, it still was very painful to listen to deposition after deposition from people I cared about. Each one failed to remember distinct instances of the mistreatment from Roger that had taken place in their presence. They still worked with him. They still interacted with him each day.

Once again, I felt expendable. My isolation grew as I slowly lost contact with colleagues that I regarded as friends. Still I held steadfast to my certainty that truth would prevail.

I think the isolation was the worst. The legal process forced me into a box where I couldn't talk about what I was experiencing. I was strictly instructed not to discuss my case with anyone other than my attorney, my treating psychiatrist and my husband.

Over time, I began to realize that some of the phone calls I received from colleagues and co-workers were no more than weak attempts to gather some sort of juicy gossip to bring back to the workplace. It was doubly devastating to discover that these old friends were not legitimately concerned about my well-being. I don't think anyone who hasn't experienced this profound darkness and isolation can ever understand the depth of pain I experienced with each waking moment.

As the legal process unfolded, one of my earliest and deeply painful lessons was the disingenuous realization that people lie. It just goes to show how trusting and, yes, naive I was. It was shocking for me to learn that people who took an oath in depositions and in courtrooms didn't take their pledge to tell the truth as seriously as I did. As my search for truth unfolded, people I thought were friends turned out to be deceivers.

The abrupt change in my work status and my personal identity was traumatic. I am a wife, a mother and a nurse. Yet, because I was broken, physically, emotionally and spiritually, I had lost a large part of my identity. A large part of me, my ego, was the fact that I was a nurse. Much of what enriched my life was my being with and caring for women in my community. I thrived and healed myself as I healed others in this role.

I had left work each night feeling satisfied because I had been able to spend that day helping other women. Whether it was a simple labor check or an absolutely back-breaking labor, I mattered because I was able to support others.

Suddenly it was all gone. Once again, I had allowed a man to control me, weaken me and take from me what I held so dear. Roger took part of my ego and part of my soul. I didn't have the life skills to recognize it as it was taking place, and I didn't I have the life skills to stop him. I could counsel patients to make sound choices, but I couldn't make sound choices for myself.

I was devastated. My life as I knew it crumbled as I fell into darkness. To make the situation worse, rumors and gossip spread through the community about my sudden departure. I sank deeper into a black hole. I was the victim of rumors, yet, I was forbidden to speak. I couldn't clarify rumors or dispel the lies, no matter what. I was forced into silence that was vital to the integrity of my legal case. I was forced to allow stupid tales to continue despite the pain they caused me. I needed to remain patient and trusting that, in the end, my truth would be heard. That was what mattered most.

I was heartbroken, ashamed and humiliated. I was unable to protect myself because I didn't have sound judgment in my arsenal.

I spent the next two years in limbo. Continuing complications from my shattered elbow prevented me from working. I was emotionally fragile and spent most days crying. I tried really hard not to be emotional in front of my children, but I couldn't always stop myself. I went to the psychiatrist every couple of weeks and would call in between scheduled appointments if I couldn't make it through. My psychiatrist, my husband, and my attorney were the only people I could speak with. So I sat at home and cried each day waiting for my next appointment with Dr. Z.

Once my attorney became involved and formal allegations were submitted to my employer, it became even more important that I abstain from sharing my story with outsiders. My family members remained unaware, and my friends were clueless. It wasn't until about a year after I stopped working when a local newspaper printed parts of the formal charges in court that some friends and many patients and coworkers learned about the lawsuit.

CHAPTER 22

Coping With Isolation

In our sessions, Dr. Z. sometimes referred to himself as the "the country shrink." I think this was his way of injecting some humor into an hour-long visit filled with some pretty painful emotions.

I began seeing Dr. Z. when Brandon was in his teenage meltdown in 2007. He was a community physician with a very good reputation. I knew him through hospital events, however I was hesitant to share the level of dysfunction in my family. But I needed help, so I took the chance.

Given his reputation, I felt he was the best person I could find to help with my family problems. I shared our drama with him and he agreed to start evaluating and treating my family. As with the treatment of any minor child, the parents will eventually become involved in the evaluative process and that was fine. Dr. Z. helped all of us to overcome Brandon's tribulations.

When I couldn't take any more abuse at work, I turned to him again.

It seemed more than fate the day I ran into Dr. Z. in the hospital hallway while I was still working there. I had been contemplating phoning him and trying to think how to broach the subject when one morning, there he was approaching me in a quiet hallway. As discreetly as possible, I tried to explain to him that I was in a very bad situation at work that involved Roger and I was feeling desperate. I recall asking him specifically if discussing this type of issue would be a problem for him because Roger was his colleague, too. I feared that perhaps Dr. Z. might not want to accept me as a patient because of the professional relationship he had with Roger. He understood my concern and stated that because he had treated me before, he had no issue that would prevent him from treating me with my current dilemma.

I also remember telling Dr. Z. that if he would not treat me, I probably would not seek care elsewhere. The thought of starting treatment with a new therapist was more than I could handle during that trying time. Dr. Z. knew my family dynamic, he knew my personal dynamic, he knew the infrastructure of the hospital I worked for and he knew Roger. I believed he was the best qualified to help me. Thankfully, he agreed. That chance meeting occurred only weeks before I left my job under the escalating hostility in my work environment.

I started treatment promptly and struggled to make it through each week until the next scheduled session. Every two weeks, Dr. Z. listened intently to my story. I felt validated. He gave me sound words of advice and allowed me to challenge his thinking when I didn't quite agree. Most importantly, he began to show me the interconnectedness between my childhood and the harassment I had endured from Roger in a way that made sense to me.

In a nutshell, I began to understand that we are not born with the skills to protect ourselves from predators. Our family members and significant role models mentor us and teach us how to recognize unhealthy situations. In my case, I was not mentored during my childhood or anytime. I had no one to teach me how to protect myself from people who mistreated me.

Quite the contrary, Dr. Z. showed me that I was not only

a victim of emotional and physical abuse as an adult, but that my entire childhood was one of persistent child abuse. I didn't have the occasional bad day growing up, I had the occasional good one.

Everyone from my mother to relatives to teachers had failed to protect me. They knocked me down every step of the way. The only person I could lean on was my father. However, my father enabled my abusers by failing to see just how bad it was for me.

By the time I reached young adulthood, I hadn't developed the internal skills to protect myself from people who meant me harm. Furthermore, one of the coping skills I developed was to "dumb down" or not be myself in order to fit in with the crowd. I so desperately wanted to fit in that I would become a chameleon just so I would be liked.

This was the norm in my work environment by the time the abuse had reached its crescendo. I was perpetually trying to "fit in" with Roger, to please him by being what he expected me to be rather than being what I truly was and who I wanted to be. Religion had been an early component of my development and religion was a factor in my abuse as well. During the course of my therapy, I developed some clarity about the negative impact religion had on me during my formative years and during my dark journey.

Therapy continued as I struggled with loneliness, depression and anxiety. I was overcome with shame and the belief that I was a profound failure as a wife and mother.

Dr. Z. counseled me and helped me to put my emotions into perspective, but those hour-long sessions passed quickly and it was in the many other hours of isolation and despair that I reflected alone.

I would go deep into my childhood and try to piece the jigsaw puzzle of my life together just like Dr. Z. did. I would try to connect events and process patterns and then bring these patterns to Dr. Z. at my next session where he would either confirm them or dismiss them with a different and frequently more accurate explanation.

In the darkness was my silence and in the silence was my lesson. I didn't know what the lesson was yet, but I knew there was a lesson for me to learn. Somewhere there was a message to feed my higher self, my divine knowing that would guide me through the darkness so that I would someday see the light.

My faithful dog, Chase endured with me during the first year of this struggle. Our family dog, the seven-year old Labrador had been my Valentine's Day gift when he was just a puppy. He was a great family dog and my loyal friend. In between therapy visits, Chase was on deck listening to me every day as I spoke out loud to him about all my troubles. He laid by me when I cried and never passed judgment on me when I felt humiliated or defeated. He provided unconditional love and companionship for hours on end when I was alone in our home and overcome with emotion.

David and my children had no idea what was happening in our house when they left for work or school, but Chase knew and it was our secret. The pain I released in his presence and the love he gave me trying to help me heal was our private time. I cherished him.

Nearly a year had passed since I left work and the legal process began. It had been a year of emotional pain and trauma, and also one of physical pain as my broken elbow was not healing according to the doctor's expectations. I had already had one surgery and was being troubled by seemingly permanent nerve damage causing pins and needles and weakness in my arm.

I left my home early one morning for my appointment with Dr. Z. I more commonly refered to these sessions as "my tune-ups," since they seemed to keep me functioning until the next appointment. I failed to notice as I left my home that a light-colored van began to follow me. By the time I had driven about eight miles of the 40-mile ride, the van began to repeatedly honk behind me and the driver was trying to motion for me to pull over. I became quite concerned that perhaps something was wrong with my car, but had no intentions of pulling over for a stranger. I continued to drive and tried to ignore the van, but the driver remained persistent and with the first opportunity pulled up along the right side of my car and held a sign on the window that said, "I'll see you in court."

I had no idea what was happening, but panic began to take over as a surge of adrenaline washed through my body. My entire body began to shake uncontrollably. I was a short distance from Dr. Z.'s office and all I could think to do was get to his office where I would be safe. For the next hour, Dr. Z. calmed me down and strongly recommended that I leave his office and contact the authorities.

I spent a few hours in the local police station trying to explain what I had just experienced and trying further to help them to understand that I was in a very unfortunate legal issue. The police made the required reports and sent me home suggesting that I be more careful of people in my surroundings and to call them if anything else happened. By the time I got home, I was emotionally drained. I was frightened and desperately fearful that my family might be in harm's way as a result of the progression of my legal action.

I let Chase out to relieve himself, unattended for just a few minutes. Less than an hour later, he collapsed in our home and began to suffer and die. Quite literally, one minute he was energetic and happy and the next he was dying. David and I rushed him to the vet, who could offer no obvious explanation for his death at that moment. Our otherwise healthy and active dog fell down and died within hours of a van being seen on my street that then followed me for several miles to intimidate me. I have my theory as to what happened. Chase is gone and nothing will bring him back.

With Chase's untimely and suspicious death, a part of me died as well. His death thrust me further into the darkness and despair. I was drowning. It was nearly one year to the day after I had left my job. The grieving made it difficult for me to inhale.

I felt responsible for Chase's death and I desperately missed the unconditional devotion he had given me each day that he was part of our family. My grief counselor and private confidante was gone. My once private grieving with only Chase as my witness was forced uncontrollably in the open as my husband and children learned to endure my anguish. My children were also suffering from the pain of losing their dear friend and childhood pet.

My house was filled with emotional suffering, pain, heartbreak and loss. I was at the epicenter.

The only other time I can recall such a time of complete loneliness is when Brandon was abducted. It was during this time that I think I felt the most defeated. I realized that I was up against an evil force that pretended to regard life as precious, but was willing to meet its own needs regardless of the cost.

CHAPTER 23

Lessons from a Country Shrink

The first year of isolation had passed and Chase had passed as well. I always thought my home was a sanctuary, a sacred space, a safe place to relax and just be.

Instead, my home had become a tomb, an above ground structure that maintained my isolation and my silence as the legal process dragged on with no end in sight. No legal representative or company executive asked to hear my truth. There was paper correspondence, but each time my attorney offered for me to speak, offers were declined.

My depression soon progressed to despair. My private sessions to which Chase had once been silent witness had unwillingly become public as my children and my husband watched me, helpless to know what to do. No one could heal my pain or soothe me through gentle words or hugs. I was inconsolable.

Yes, it was the loss of Chase, but it was something more. I knew I was losing myself.

As I embarked on my second year of isolation, I turned more inwardly to prayer. I began to process and critically evaluate from my childhood forward the connection of my religious experiences and how they contributed to who I had become.

I had very few memories of my childhood or my previous marriage. It seemed that once I overcame those challenges, I closed the doors forever on many of those memories. Yes, I had complete clarity on my childhood abuses and my son's abduction. Certain painful exits on my life's roadmap remained clear, but in my despondency it seemed that my religious experiences, good and bad, were being brought forth in my consciousness to direct me and maybe, just maybe, to heal me.

I was born and raised Roman Catholic, so Catholicism was my childhood foundation. It spoke to me through my developmental years. I attended Catholic school where I received a sound private education that in the 1970s far surpassed our local public elementary schools. However, the emotional damage that came with the antiquated parochial tradition served much more harm than good.

My school was primarily attended by upper middle-class children. I was one of three poor children in a class of 18 students. We were together from kindergarten through eighth grade with little variation in class size along the way. Being poor is not easy, but being poor and being constantly reminded of it by teachers and nuns was frankly humiliating and intended to be so.

My parents were not benefactors to the church, nor did they participate in the PTA. As a matter of fact, my tuition was paid through my father's physical labor. He was a painter by trade and would barter his painting services as a means to keep his daughters in private school. He painted the church and the rectory during my academic studies at this school. As much as I love him for this wonderful sacrifice, he had no understanding of the emotional scarring that was occurring in that building that he thought provided me and my sister with a protective and nurturing academic and religious environment.

My elementary years are filled with memories of being called hurtful names by the school principal. Sr. C. referred to me as "fat" on occasion and one of my classmates frequently called me Ms. Piggy. I can recall favoritism amongst teachers for the children of the wealthiest families and the overwhelming desire to fit in, but knowing that I didn't.

I do not regret these memories, though. It is with these experiences that I grew. I worked hard to overcome and to be like the more affluent kids around me. By no means do I wish to offend Catholics or suggest these experiences are common in the Catholic faith. I simply speak of the foundation that my faith was based upon as a means to show the evolution that has occurred in my life's journey.

After elementary school, I convinced my father that I really wanted to go to a public high school. I think he was relieved deep down since he would now be released from the burden of figuring out how to pay for my next four years. I did okay in public school. I was a regular teen girl and I felt like I "fit in." I was surrounded by rich, middle-class and poor kids, so I didn't stand out in the crowd.

I stopped going to church regularly, but I still believed in God. I believed I was watched by my own guardian angel. Most important was a fundamental belief that my life had a "higher purpose" that really developed during these years. Sure, I partied and took risks like most teens, but by the end of those four years, my purpose refocused on religion and my faith.

As I struggled with my identity and partying with friends seemed to be unfulfilling, my path led to a local evangelical church. It was an Assembly of God church, to be precise. I was invited there by the parents of the boy I had once dated. It was where I met Gavin and the whole chain of painful events around our marriage began to unfold.

I loved being welcomed by his family and feeling like I was included in what, from my perspective, was "normal." It was the early 1980s and my parents were long separated. I lived with my dad and my sister lived with our mom. I pretty much continued to raise myself and tried to remain a positive influence on my sister while she struggled with her identity as well.

My mother was bartending and mixing prescription pills with alcohol on a regular basis. She dated around and each time she met a new guy she liked, my sister and I would become her last priority. I can remember visiting her one weekend and she was having a new guy come over to see her. She gave me specific instructions to go outside to play and pretend like I didn't know her. When I questioned her motive, the response was chilling. I was told that she didn't want him to know she had a daughter my age. The words cut through me: I was once again rejected by my mother. It was the last weekend I visited.

My father was busy "sowing his oats" with his crowd of friends. He spent weekends partying, doing cocaine, drinking and "making up for lost time," as he described it.

I spent most weekends alone, unsupervised, finding my own trouble until I found the evangelical church. After that "conversion," I attended service each Sunday, went to Bible study groups during the week and really started to assimilate in the group and feel welcome. I enjoyed the palpable spirit that is felt in the service and the genuine feeling of fellowship that was shared at this local church.

I met Gavin when I went to see a southern gospel group perform one evening. I found him to be handsome with a Southern innocence that was attractive to me. We were instantly smitten with each other. I was just 16. From that moment forward, we began a long distance courtship. In less than two years, I was married and moving South.

Life on the road with a gospel singing group is an eye opener of huge proportions. I was a barely 18 years old and a newlywed who left her home and her past in an attempt to start fresh. I was baptized in the spirit of the Pentecostal

Church and full of ambition and desire of a new Christian life. Gavin travelled with the group about three weeks a month. They toured by bus and their schedule was planned almost a year in advance. I would drive to nearby cities or states to spend a few days with him and play my role of a new wife. That time was an adventure and I met hundreds of truly lovely and inspirational Christian people who loved God and loved each other. They were innocent people who gave generously of themselves and their paychecks as the donation plate was passed around "for the grace of God" by the group that employed Gavin. Little did these people know that the money they so freely gave was not being used for the intentions they were being led to believe. There were no planned and upcoming trips to the Holy Land. There were no mass Bible distributions to Third World countries. The generous people of all these wonderful communities were being hoaxed. I was dumbfounded.

I recall Gavin justifying the work being done as good work and making excuses for the deceptions to the churchgoers. I was naïve. I just accepted what was being done and kept my mouth shut. In retrospect, I realize now this was just another attempt to "fit in."

Eventually, the band members (Gavin's employers) began to complain about my presence at their concerts. It was not because I was disruptive or a distraction to Gavin, rather it was because they were concerned that I would return to their hometown and share stories with their wives about their mistresses and sexual liaisons on tour. So, after a few months of travelling to meet up with my husband, I was banned from their lifestyle. I don't think they ever realized I was aware of the financial misappropriations as well.

Within the year, Gavin was "let go" from his job with the band. They group cited financial reasons, however their fear of my growing friendship with their wives and daughters was the true reason.

Religion left a bad taste in my mouth after that. I stopped going to church, stayed away from the Bible and just moved at my own pace. I never stopped believing in God until Brandon challenged my faith more than I could handle in his late teenage crisis. The hypocrisy I witnessed was becoming more public by the late 1980s when evangelical leaders like Jim Bakker and Jimmy Swaggart were held accountable for their sexual and fiscal indiscretions.

Raising my children, I tried to put the good faith effort into attending church and building a religious foundation for each of them to develop. I tried the Presbyterian and Methodist faiths and even bounced back to my old Evangelical church for a few Sunday services. But hypocrisy rested in the back of my mind and I no longer felt I could find God through organized religion.

I have never believed there is one religion that reigns supreme to all others. My heart tells me that each faith is equally important and there are many paths available to the Divine/ Creator/God. I think this evolution of faith comes from my many years as a nurse experiencing illness, wellness, birth and death in the multitude of faiths that coexist. I recall my basic-level nursing program teaching the students over and over again the importance of not bringing your personal cultural and religious belief systems into the care of patients. That point resonated with me from the first moment I learned it. It is not for me to pass judgment or give advice on care based on my philosophy, religion, or culture. Each of us must draw conclusions that fit our needs. It makes perfect sense to me, but unfortunately so many organized religions can't accept that notion.

So as I have matured as a person, I have also matured in spirit. I don't disrespect religions of any kind, but for me the best fit is with the one-on-one connection I have with the Divine/ Creator/God that lives within me and *is* me. It is through my despondency in those years at home, away from the work I loved, that this self-knowledge came forth.

Interwoven in my despondency was my job as mother. That job was becoming more challenging as I sank deeper into darkness.

"Mom, I have a stomach ache," I heard one afternoon as Danny joined me on the front porch where I was sitting in the afternoon sun reflecting on my life and the legal drama that consumed my attention along with my fear of failure and letting down my family.

"Where does it hurt, baby?" I asked. I still called him "Baby" sometimes, despite what others may say, even though Danny was 11 years old and my youngest. He will always be Mama's baby. I spent a few minutes assessing his symptoms and gave my expert treatment advice: "Go try to fart and that should make it better."

Of course he agreed, being a young boy and having some experience with this as well as the 11-year-old obsession with humorous bodily processes.

He sat with me for a little bit and tried to shake off the discomfort while we waited for his dad to come home from work. It was the first day of David's vacation and we were going to go for a drive and then out to eat. As the sun shone down on a beautiful day, the humidity seemed to be breaking and just a few clouds skipped through the bright blue sky. We waited for David's return and that one big fart of relief for Danny's aching stomach.

By early evening, the stomach pain persisted and my little guy was just trying to tolerate it. Recognizing that this was no simple stomach ache, I started assessing him further and began to fear the alternate diagnosis: a hot appendix.

By 5 p.m., I called his doctor and asked if I could bring him for a visit. We are fortunate in our community to have good access to medical care. Our pediatrician's office is open most nights till 8 p.m. and that night we needed to make use of it

As I was on the phone explaining Danny's symptoms to the receptionist, I heard a cry for help coming from the family room. I turned around to see my son just a foot away from the bathroom door, vomiting all over the carpet.

"Damn!" was my first thought. I felt terrible that he was starting to vomit, but of course I was trying to process the situation.

"How am I going to get this puke off the floor?" I wondered. Hanging up the phone, I led him into the bathroom and simultaneously try to keep our new puppy, Tater, away from the mess.

"David!" I screamed. "I need your help!"

We scrambled to clean the carpet, monitor Danny and prepare to leave for the doctor's office.

"It looks like we have appendicitis," Dr. C. calmly broke the news to my squirming son. His eyes opened wide as he fought to hold back his tears. My husband may have been a little bit surprised by the news, but I was already pretty sure of my diagnosis and was making mental preparations for the next step. It took a few more minutes to complete some lab work, followed by a stressful conversation about which hospital to go to.

Pediatric cases in our region often go to a larger medical facility about 100 miles away. Dr. C. advised that if it was her child, she would go there. However, I didn't feel comfortable travelling that far. It is an outstanding teaching facility, yet I was unsettled with the thought of the accompanying flood of residents, interns and other various medical students who would be practicing on my son. To add to my dismay, this appendix issue was occurring in the month of July. Rule number one on teaching hospitals: Avoid them in July. This is when the influx of new residents takes place and it is statistically when the most patient mistakes occur. So, my inner voice was screaming to me, "Stay local."

Thank God my husband agreed.

Confirmation of appendicitis was completed with a CT scan and two more hours of waiting while Danny writhed in pain. As I sat and watched my son and his hot appendix simmering, I prayed relentlessly that he didn't start to boil. A boil could land us in much more than a routine procedure. Danny was in the operating room by 2:40 a.m. and in the recovery room 40 minutes later. Surgery was textbook smooth. We could exhale and Danny could begin to heal.

Despite my 20 years in the field, the advancements of medicine truly still amaze me. When I first became a nurse, most patients with appendectomies had a hospital stay of about four days. Danny was in the recovery room at 3:30 a.m. and home watching cartoons by 11:30 a.m. I could not have asked for a better outcome.

CHAPTER 24

Crazy Days, Crazy Years

*A*s any parent knows, raising three children is no easy task, especially when they are teenagers. The struggles of the teenage years can be overwhelming for both parents and children. I suppose my lack of sufficient coping mechanisms, in addition to my prolonged emotional turmoil from an endless legal battle, compounded my despair.

One day, during my time of isolation, Celeste got on my last nerve. It was a wake-up call for me and helped me realize how unstable I was becoming.

Celeste was a typical 16-year old girl, complete with attitude. When I asked her a simple question, she responded with a tone that implied she was doing me a wonderful favor by even acknowledging that I spoke to her. It is a common teenage malady and a more common parental complaint, but on that day it pushed all of my buttons.

Celeste was playing volleyball with friends and I needed to contact her, so I called her phone. No answer. Not once, not twice, but three times over about 20 minutes. Still no answer.

I was livid. In our house, the children have the privilege of having cell phones with the clear understanding that when parents call, they answer without excuse. That wasn't the first time that Celeste failed to answer when I called.

Thirty minutes passed before she returned my call. I instructed her to come home immediately. When she arrived, I demanded her cell phone. She refused. She wanted to know why and just flat out refused. This dialogue lasted about ten minutes with my frustration turning to rage.

My throat began to hurt from the screaming. My anger was evident, the message was clear, yet my daughter simply laughed at me and said she was not giving me the phone. She called me "crazy" and a few other choice words that now escape me. She must have had a brief moment of clarity after the twelfth time I screamed for her to give me the f***ing phone because she finally handed it over to me. Unfortunately, for her and the phone it was too late.

I threw that phone down the staircase to the lower level of the house where it landed on the tile floor and broke into six or seven pieces.

Was I crazy at that moment? Probably.

Well, she called David, angry and upset and reported that I threw the phone for no good reason. NO GOOD REASON! In my mind, I didn't need a better reason. Yes, I threw the phone. I was enraged. My daughter was disrespecting me and I reached my limit. I am not sure if that justifies a diagnosis of crazy.

On the contrary, I can honestly say that at the moment Celeste handed me her phone, I had a choice to make given my state of rage. I could, first, throw the phone. I could, second, manually remove a couple of her teeth for disrespecting me. I chose the first for the obvious reason that I won't hit my child, but also because it would be less expensive to replace the phone. I was out of control and it was a bad day. It was the kind of day where I just wanted to go to bed and wake up to a fresh new start. Unfortunately for me, that fresh new start was never on the horizon. I was failing to cope.

Before we went to bed, Celeste, David, and I discussed the events and everyone's viewpoints were heard. We may not have agreed with each other, but we listened. I try not to let days end without telling each of my children and my husband that I love them.

Tomorrow would be better. Or would it?

Each morning when I first open my eyes and process the moment, it takes a few minutes to go back in time and remember the good or the bad that I went to sleep with.

The next day, I prepared to start on a positive note and let the teenage attitude become a memory. I hoped Celeste would wake up in a better place as well.

All seemed okay as I set out in the morning for a manicure, a personal treat. That brief retreat was my time that allowed me to step out of darkness in my attempt to heal. The goal was to make it home without smudging a nail and to make it at least three days without chipping one. For active women, this is no easy task and some may perceive as simply not possible. But, I hoped for the best and looked forward to getting out of my tomb.

All was well as I returned home, anticipating the soup in my refrigerator and remembering that it was past noon and I had yet to eat. No smudges as I gently pulled out a pot from the kitchen cabinet. I started the soup on the stove and headed upstairs to my bedroom to grab a sweater. At that same moment, I heard frantic cries from Brandon in the main bathroom.

"Mom, come quick!" he screamed.

I tried to dismiss him and his never-ending melodrama and responded calmly, "What, Brandon?"

More panic set in as he screamed, "Mom, really, come now!"

At that very instant I turned to see what had him so upset and looked down on the floor to see a rolling current of dirty, nasty toilet water approaching my feet.

"OH, MY GOD!! What is going on??" I shouted.

The next few moments seemed drag out forever while water flowed freely over the toilet rim and into the hallway and adjoining upstairs bedrooms.

"Open the door!" I screamed as I tried to enter the bathroom and avoid stepping on loosely flowing feces nearby.

"Mom what do I do?" Brandon asked me in panic and stood staring at the toilet bowl much like a deer in the headlights.

"All I did was flush and this happened," he said helplessly.

As seconds raced by, I grabbed towels from the closet and started throwing them down to catch the current. Next, I went to hall closet to grab the plunger. OH, DEAR GOD PLEASE LET IT BE THERE! One plunge, two plunges. Success! The welcome sound of water going down the drain and further disaster averted.

Oh, shit! Literally.

"Celeste," I yelled downstairs. "Turn off my soup so it doesn't catch on fire!"

She thankfully obliged me, leaving the teenage attitude for another day.

Disaster under control or was it? Brandon was going to be late for school and he would need to shower in a room $1/4$-inch deep in toilet water. I needed to clean, but had no idea where to begin. The dog was walking through feces water looking for the best morsel to eat . . .

Eat! I was starving. After all, I'm a nurse and bodily excretions are no strangers to me. But there wasn't a moment to spare.

First things first. I dried up the bulk of the water with towels. Second, grabbed the dog and prepared to throw him in the bath after Brandon finished. Third, disinfect, disinfect, disinfect. There comes a time when nothing is clean enough. I started the washer with the unending pile of dirty towels, washed the floor, cleaned the carpet and finished by washing myself. An hour later it seemed that the disaster was resolved.

Finally, I could enjoy my soup. As I stood in front of the stove re-heating my breakfast/lunch, I glanced into our formal living room and made mental note of what appeared to be doggy pee-pee on my white carpet. As I went to assess the next problem, I soon discovered it was not doggy pee-pee, rather toilet bowl water dripping through the ceiling.

I yelled in my loudest voice, "HOW MUCH MORE DO YOU EXPECT ME TO DEAL WITH, GOD?" shaking my head in despair, tears streaming down my face. I prepared to clean the next mess, resigning myself to another delayed lunch.

All disasters resolved and I hadn't chipped a nail. I am woman, hear me roar! By the time I got to my soup it kind of looked like everything I just cleaned. So I made a sandwich instead. Maybe I was coping a little better than I thought I was.

CHAPTER 25

Where Is My Normal?

As the days of my isolation slowly turned into years, it was by the grace of God that my family remained basically stable. Brandon had made significant emotional improvements and brought himself through his personal issues successfully. Celeste and Danny were usually pleasant, and thriving in their academics, sports and musical talents. Once again David was burdened by being primary caregiver to the children as well as treading lightly with my fragile emotional state.

At the same time Chase died, I was preparing emotionally for Brandon to study abroad in Europe for a semester. Brandon successfully completed community college and was transferring to state college and would be off to Europe. The thought of my firstborn being ready to leave home and be independent for four months was difficult for me to accept in addition to the other struggles I was facing. I was thrilled for Brandon and very proud of his overcoming anxiety as well as learning albeit the "hard way" that manipulative behavior doesn't work in a grown-up world. In addition, I was very proud of his adventuresome spirit as he faced new challenges and new journeys in a foreign land. But, as he was preparing for his new adventures I was also sad that his departure would further silence my home with one less child living there. I continued my daily ritual of shedding tears and pain as I maintained the vigil in my tomb, looking for some basic understanding of how my life seemed to be so wrong.

My consistent therapy with Dr. Z. led to a diagnosis of Post-Traumatic Stress Disorder (PTSD). PTSD is a phenomenon that may occur as a result of some unforeseen trauma. It is more common in people with underlying anxiety from their past. I have always acknowledged and respected the disorder and the devastating effect it can have on people. However, I had never thought of myself as being a potential victim of such a disorder. In my mind, PTSD is reserved for military personnel and victims of tragic events such as rape. But, the behaviors I was exhibiting were consistent with my diagnosis despite my reluctance to accept it.

I had reached my lowest point. David was reporting to Dr. Z. and me the erratic and irrational behavior that I was exhibiting. There were things I wasn't recognizing I was doing. I would fly off the handle at the simplest stressors. I was not sleeping. I was crying all the time in front of my children. I was distancing myself from my immediate family, not returning phone calls and generally avoiding contact with others. Although, David was trying to remain patient and explain to me that I was not acting appropriately, I would become more hostile toward him and accusatory. I told him many times that he was unsympathetic and judgmental. It sucked.

From the depths of this darkness, it was a routine physical with my long-time primary care physician that opened a door for me and marked the beginning of my healing process. He recommended a meeting with a wonderful spiritual counselor and gave me her contact information. I certainly don't view this appointment with him as accidental. I see it clearly as divine intervention.

I called Claire and scheduled a meeting with a renewed sense of hope. We never discussed details of my legal action. We focused our visits on strengthening my spiritual foundation, meditation techniques and energy balancing through Reiki.

Claire helped me to reconnect with my higher self, my intuitive knowing. It was through this teaching that my personal trust began to grow and I was able to accomplish forgiveness at all levels.

It was during that time I became mama to our brand-new puppy, Tater. When we brought him home as our new family pet, he was a two-pound Yorkie no bigger than Danny's sneaker. Tater brought instant joy to all of us after we had suffered so much with the loss of Chase. For me Tater had a more profound purpose: He was my new angel, a gift from the Divine that was given to me after suffering from repetitive heartbreak. Tater brought joy back into my life. I could love and nurture and watch this new little life grow and learn during a time when I felt withered and barren.

Early on in my healing journey, I learned the importance of daily meditation to ground and balance myself as a means of preparing for what the day may bring. This meditation does not have to be for a long period of time. In the beginning, sitting in silence and clearing my thoughts for five minutes was a challenge. Learning how to empty an unnaturally cluttered mind is a process that requires patience. I now sit in meditation for about 20 minutes a day, longer if I am so inspired. I do not perceive time in my meditation process. It just becomes what feels right for that moment.

Each day when I begin my meditation, I set forth my clear intentions for the day. This process allows me to be an active participant in my life, rather than a passive victim of circumstance. My intention each and every day is "to know my enlightened nature that I may benefit all beings."

I will also add anything that inspires me for that day. Whether I'm setting forth my intention to be a more patient mother or setting forth my intention to eliminate fear from a situation, I am the creator of my journey and with this journey will come personal challenges that I will forever be more prepared to overcome. Each day as it comes I intend to consciously connect with all of life and be a positive contributor to the greater good.

By beginning my day, setting forth my intentions, and grounding myself through meditation, I have learned to allow the Divine/God energy that I believe in to not only work through me, but more importantly *be* me.

Through this spiritual work and continued therapy with Dr. Z., I became much more perceptive to the patterns of dysfunction from my past and the similarities in my present. But understanding and recognizing patterns does not eliminate the emotions that these patterns invoke in my being.

Resentment toward my mother became much more unsettling when I realized that she was motivated by manipulation, not true illness. As old feelings re-surfaced, I began to struggle more with anger toward my mother. I needed to come to terms with these periodic recurring emotions in order to transcend the resentment and anger, thereby allowing self-healing.

I spent several years blaming myself for Brandon's abduction. I believed that if I hadn't hurt Gavin, then he wouldn't have hurt me. This was flawed thinking. Gavin was unable to accept that I didn't love him and didn't want to be married to him. As a result of his poor coping skills, he manipulated me into staying with him and caused unspeakable trauma to our son through his abduction. Rather than accepting and coming to terms with what could have been an amicable divorce, he chose to manipulate me more by taking my son from me. The message he was sending was, "If I can't have you then you can't have Brandon".

This is supported by the fact that Gavin gave me back my

son when he thought I had returned to our marriage. Unfortunately, the consequence of this extremely poor choice has to this day cost Gavin his relationship with his son.

Steve let me know that if I continued my pregnancy against his wishes, then I was on my own. It was an embarrassing situation for me to overcome, but he could not manipulate my behavior that time.

I spent the majority of my lifetime being manipulated and conversely learning how to manipulate. My mother was a strong role model for manipulative behavior and I learned well. With David, it wasn't that he was manipulating me; it was the opposite. I had become so full of my own ego and inflated personal expectations that I manipulated him to get what I wanted. As a result, our marriage nearly crumbled and I nearly lost the most important person in my life.

In my forced isolation, I turned to prayer. I prayed for direction. I prayed for healing. I prayed for strength for my family, my patients, but most importantly I began to pray for those who had caused me harm. My dark journey became an intense exploration into the whys and hows of my life. I have heard that out of our darkest moments can come the most brilliant rays of light if we choose to do the work required to gain understanding.

When I shattered my elbow in a frantic exit from a patient's room, I never could have imagined the personal and spiritual growth that would follow. I never would have imagined that I could reach such a personal low moment and still have the resolve to overcome and become a better person than when I started. But, that is what this journey has become. And it is work. Sometimes it is more work than I would like, but I remain committed to this challenge.

My life has its share of trauma and has not at all been ordinary. I had a lot to work through and process as I recognized that healing for me required forgiveness at many different levels.

CHAPTER 26

Seeking Direction
Through My Higher Self

More than two years passed before I was called for my deposition in the lawsuit against my former employers. As my isolation continued, so did my challenge to overcome the depression, pain and the sense of being utterly alone.

I was in physical pain every day from my elbow injury, which still had not healed, but had not yet been classified as permanent. A local newspaper had printed an article about my legal action without regard for my privacy. I had been followed by a strange vehicle, buried my dog and continued to be flabbergasted by a legal process that would lose a race with a snail. After all that had transpired, it was finally my time to speak in the preliminary proceeding that would determine if my case ever went to trial.

I had never been deposed before, but my attorney had forewarned me that I would leave the event feeling like the rape victim who was to blame because her skirt was "too short."

This is not an inaccurate analogy. It was grueling, humiliating and exhausting. After this experience, I can understand how an innocent person might confess to murder after the nine hours of questioning like I endured. I was made to feel like I was the perpetrator rather than the victim. To say that the defense attorneys treated me like shit doesn't do them justice for just how low they can sink.

I was trained in nursing. In nursing, it is my utmost goal and priority to help my patient. Nursing and law are counterintuitive. In nursing, we are trained in the art and science of healing and to cause no harm. This is termed non-maleficence.

In law, the attorneys are being paid to do whatever it takes to win the case. Right and wrong are not in their vocabulary; they are completely focused on victory. They are going to cause harm in order to protect their client, guilty or not, culpable or not. The attorneys are not concerned with the other's party's emotional or physical state. Non-maleficence is not in the lawyer's vocabulary. It is all about the win, regardless of the damage caused to the other party.

Before the day of the deposition, I called Shana, one of my closest friends and asked her to lead a prayer circle to help strengthen my spirit before I faced the defending attorneys.

My sister attended the prayer circle, along with a small group of friends that who had no idea I was involved in a lawsuit until the local newspaper printed my story. Remember my attorneys had imposed a strict order of silence on me. The prayer circle gathered at my home a few days before my deposition. I am still overwhelmed with joy at the love and support my friends showed me. A prayer circle puts forth the request of the person who requests it. I was seeking a time of prayer and an immersion in the positive love energy of friendship. Shana led the circle with her unique spiritual wisdom and guided me through the process.

Shana and I became friends when we met in nursing school many years ago. We learned how to be nurses together and we supported each other through relationship and parenting struggles. Together we nurtured the Divine Feminine within ourselves and helped support and facilitate our personal growth.

As my friends and I gathered, Shana led the blessings and announced my intentions for gathering in prayer.

My intentions for this gathering were:

TO HONOR MY VOICE
TO SPEAK MY TRUTH
TO OVERCOME FEAR AND MAINTAIN CLARITY

We prayed as a group for my protection and to help me to clearly speak my truth. I felt as prepared as I possibly could be given my lack of experience with the legal process.

As the prayer circle ended, I felt blanketed in white love energy, filled with strength and ready to face any negativity that would come my way. I remained thankful that I had dear friends who would support me and take time out of their busy schedules to join me in this ritual.

On the day of the deposition, my attorney had instructed me to wait for the question to be asked in its entirety before I answered and to answer only the question asked. It sounded simple, but it was not easy. Nearly two years had passed and that was the first time anyone involved with my former employer was going to hear my truth. I had been holding in every ounce of pain and emotion within my being for all that time. My biggest fear was that from the first moment I could finally speak, I might not be able to stop. I did my best.

Despite the hospital's attorneys' best effort to get me to fumble my story, I stood firm. I cried hysterically at times. I yelled back a little bit. They tried their best to demean and humiliate me, but I stood firm. Six hours passed and the inquisition was over. Yet, it wasn't over. The attorneys broke for a late lunch and returned to grill me for three more hours. My inquisition ended and I was drained.

During my legal humiliation, it is important to mention that the opposing attorneys felt it was necessary to have me admit that I don't wear panties. This was not a secret of mine since coworkers and I often discussed our private choices and many women do not wear panties. The attorneys chose to take this tidbit of my personal information and twist it into some sort of defective risqué behavior that they believed would discredit me in some way. Somehow my admission that I do not wear panties was a way to excuse Roger's harassment and my employer's responsibility to have acted more expeditiously. To put this in simpler terms, they were flat out saying the sexual harassment was my fault. If I wore panties, maybe this wouldn't have happened. How ridiculous!

Nine cumulative hours of questioning was finally over. I was raw, emotionally drained and shattered from the repeated accusation that I brought Roger's behavior on myself. That was just how the opposing attorneys wanted me to feel. Nevertheless, I had stood up to the accusations and defended my position. No matter what, I spoke my truth. Depositions of all witnesses lasted for several more months with all questioning ending two and one-half years after I left my job. Roger remained hospital staff.

During a woman's labor process, when the fetal head begins to stretch and thin the perineum in preparation for the inevitable delivery, there is an intense fiery burning sensation. This burning sensation is unlike any other pain described during an injury. The relentless pressure of the fetal head stretching open the vagina from finger-width to the width of a full size baby's head creates hyperactive nerve impulses that rapidly transmit this fiery hot sensation and can make a woman feel like she is being ripped in two. This experience has long been identified as the "ring of fire."

My dear friend, Helena, called my painful, surreal experience in the nine hours of deposition my own personal "ring of fire." Despite the lawyers' taunting, the accusations that I deserved Roger's unwelcome attentions and their efforts to make me feel like a whore, I survived. Unquestionably, I was battered by the experience, but I survived.

CHAPTER 27

Lessons to Be Shared

*M*y survival involves daily prayer and meditation. Healing comes as I learn anew each day to forgive myself. Self-forgiveness is much more difficult than forgiving others.

Spiritual growth is unique to each individual's belief system. There is no single right or wrong way to approach spiritual growth. The prayer and meditation that I have developed from my cultural background along with the spiritual mentors who came into my life have been key in helping me to cope, to resolve my pain and to heal.

Some days are better than others. I have not had a miraculous healing; dark days return without warning. This is part of being human. Through the steps I constructed from a variety of sources that I like to call *The Forgiveness Factor,* I have journeyed through darkness and taken both baby steps and giant steps toward personal healing.

There are different types of forgiveness that are vital for spiritual, emotional and physical healing.

First is the ability to forgive another for the hurt that has been caused. This is accomplished by consciously identifying the hurt, acknowledging the lesson it has brought, then developing the ability to release that hurt and no longer harbor it within one's being. For me, I systematically and painstakingly itemized the hurt I felt from childhood to the present and thanked each hurtful moment for the lessons I learned. Forgiveness was possible when I released the hurt because it no longer served a purpose.

The next type of forgiveness is the recognition that we may cause pain in others and that we need to release the personal pain that comes from creating this pain. I caused David so much pain over the years, and owning this was tremendously difficult. I had manipulated and lied as I sought personal gratification at the expense of my partner. I needed to acknowledge that I am capable of causing others pain in order to properly receive forgiveness from David and myself.

With *The Forgiveness Factor,* I learned how to identify what would move me forward on my path of personal healing. I created a list of the people and circumstances I needed to forgive and systematically worked through the process as follows:

1. Identify the people who have caused me pain and why I feel this pain.

2. Identify the pain I feel from others and consciously release it to the universe in a personal ritual.

3. Allow myself to forgive those who have caused me pain as a means to my physical, emotional and spiritual healing.

4. Identify the people I have caused pain and recognize why I caused them pain.

5. Identify the pain that I caused others with my actions.

6. Allow myself forgiveness for the pain I have caused others as a means to my physical, emotional and spiritual healing.

Forgiving others for the pain or hurt that they have intentionally caused is no easy task. Human nature steps in and wants to interfere with the forgiveness process. The Old Testament speaks of "an eye for an eye." Most of us can identify with that. But then Jesus came along in the New Testament and undid retaliation and spoke of "turning the other cheek." Jesus' philosophy is far less palatable in terms of human nature's desire for revenge for perceived wrongs. Yet, by allowing positive energy to flow throughout my being without impediment, I learned to release hurt caused by others and become open to the idea of forgiveness.

For me, learning how to forgive family members, past relationships, Roger and the hospital executives was vital to my healing.

In a step-by-step method, I identified the hurt that each person caused me and why it was painful for me to experience. This identification gave me validity. The pain I felt was real and deserved to be acknowledged.

Next, I consciously labeled the feeling and released it to the universe. I wrote it on paper and burned it in a personal ceremony or I spoke the words out loud and blew them away never to be seen again. But this process of ritualistic release of the pain, rage and fear made it possible for me to find closure and allowed my healing process to begin.

Five years have passed and my legal drama ended in defeat. On more than one occasion I was offered a financial settlement to avoid a jury trial. On more than one occasion I declined. Money was not the motivating factor that initiated my legal action. Money was not going to heal my wounds.

Legal closure came when the court decided that I had not reported my alleged harassment in a timely manner. I had waited too long.

You see the legal system does not consider human emotions and the fact that victims feel powerless and are often unable to promptly report abuse. Victims do not operate within a framework of legal statute of limitations; rather they struggle to just get through each day. In addition, many victims do not even recognize that they are indeed being victimized.

So I did not have my day in court. I did not get to tell my story. I continue to live in pain every day from an injury from which I will never fully recover. I am challenged by Post-Traumatic Stress Disorder. My healing comes through the steps I developed in *The Forgiveness Factor.*

I share with you the many hats that I wear and the hats we all wear. These are the hats that once I identified helped me to regain personal control.

From the day of our birth, we become daughters or sons. We grow in our families and our tribes and develop according to their particular belief systems. Some of us feel complete in this system and others will alter or modify according to what feels right for them.

Many of us follow the path of becoming a spouse and/or a parent, not necessarily in that order, like me.

To date, I have become a daughter, a sister, a wife, a mother, a nurse, an ex-wife, a mother again, a wife again and a mother again. Of course, scattered throughout these hats are the interim hats of occasional girlfriend and ex-girlfriend. I find it sad that some people regret some of the hats they have worn and wish they could change a piece of their past experiences. For me, each of these hats tells my story. I wouldn't change a sentence.

My legal journey ended with its assault on my character and its challenge to the fortitude of my spirit. However, I choose not to identify myself as a victim regardless of the diagnoses that I have been given by the experts. To continue to be a victim would be allowing those who caused me harm to continue to steal my power.

I will no longer give my power to another being or another situation. Yes, I was a victim. I was a victim more than one time in my life. It may be said that I spent most of my life being a victim in some regard, but no more.

I am in control now. I went through the ring of fire and birthed myself anew. Yes, there are some significant burns and scars, but today I have been tempered like steel. Today I am a wiser and more powerful woman. Today, I can honor myself and look toward the future with confidence and strength. I no longer wear a mask of normal. I embrace the true person I am.

About the Author

This story is written under a pseudonym to maintain the anonymity of those who would prefer to not be identified. The author no longer works as a nurse, but she continues to advocate for nursing issues, including workplace safety. She and David continue to raise their three children and through their sustained love and commitment for each other, they have grown closer over the years.